CLASSROOM MANAGEMENT
matters

The Social–Emotional
Learning Approach
Children Deserve

Gianna Cassetta
Brook Sawyer

HEINEMANN
Portsmouth, NH

Heinemann

361 Hanover Street

Portsmouth, NH 03801–3912

www.heinemann.com

Offices and agents throughout the world

Library of Congress Cataloging-in-Publication Data

Cassetta, Gianna.

   Classroom management matters : the social–emotional learning approach children deserve / Gianna Cassetta and Brook Sawyer.

      pages cm

   Includes bibliographical references.

   ISBN 978-0-325-06182-5

   1. Classroom management—Social aspects. 2. Inclusive education.   I. Sawyer, Brook.   II. Title.

LB3013.C37 2015

371.102'4—dc23   2015011625

Editor: Margaret LaRaia

Developmental editor: Alan Huisman

Production: Vicki Kasabian and Patty Adams

Cover design: Suzanne Heiser

Interior design: Shawn Girsberger

Typesetter: Shawn Girsberger

Manufacturing: Steve Bernier

Printed in the United States of America on acid-free paper

19 18 17 16 15 EBM 1 2 3 4 5

To my first teachers:

Mom, for teaching me that fair isn't always equal: every child has different needs.
Dad, for teaching me that you don't just hope for equity; you have to take a stand.

—Gianna

To Janet Miltenberger:

May every child know a teacher who cherishes and inspires him, and may every parent have such an ally as she has been to me.

—Brook

Contents

Foreword by Carmen Fariña

All educators believe that children should be accountable for their behavior and supported as they learn from their mistakes, but what does that look like in practice? In school districts across the country, superintendents, principals, and teachers attempt to answer this question. In *Classroom Management Matters: The Social–Emotional Learning Approach Children Deserve* you'll find an answer that makes sense and feels achievable. The authors, Gianna Cassetta, an experienced classroom teacher, principal, and coach, and Brook Sawyer, an education researcher, show us that building meaningful relationships with one's students is the foundation for helping them develop social–emotional competency and creating a positive school culture in which all students have the opportunity to thrive. These relationships must be compassionate as well as firm and must take place in a structured environment in which students know what is expected of them, receive positive feedback when they meet expectations, and are given multiple opportunities to learn the social–emotional skills they need—both in and out of school. This is a refreshing approach, offering pedagogy backed by methodology.

I particularly like the authors' insistence that we rethink our use of the word "control." While we cannot always "control" behavior, we can help children learn self-awareness and self-management. When students see that a struggling student is supported and shown how to do better, they see that their own negative behaviors do not define them but instead provide information and the opportunity to learn better ways of being. We can foster students' social awareness and teach them the skills they need to enjoy and maintain positive relationships with others.

We can provide them with guidance and practice so that they learn responsible decision making.

In the New York City public schools we are working diligently to create school communities that embrace a youth development approach to student behavior. To this end, we have infused social–emotional learning into our professional development for school staff so that their work with students focuses on prevention as well as supportive interventions. In the same way, our Respect for All Program promotes interpersonal and intergroup respect with the goal of preventing bullying and/or bias-based behavior. We are deeply committed to building a safe and supportive community within each classroom and within each school as a whole. Our obligation as educators is to provide our students with a nurturing environment and an inclusive framework that supports each student's progress.

For too long, our school and classroom communities have been highly compartmentalized, as if the eight hours a day children spend with us are only for learning content areas—math, science, social studies, and language arts. This compartmentalization has meant that we have not allowed ourselves or our children to be fully human in school. Often, we have not acknowledged that children make mistakes and need to be given the opportunity and support to do better.

As this accessible book makes clear, good classroom management requires patience and a commitment to each individual child in our care. The path to a positive school culture is paved not through force but through shared experiences, clear expectations, a true understanding of the kinds of needs that shape students' misbehavior, and the social–emotional skills they need to meet behavioral expectations.

Perhaps most importantly, success depends upon the willingness of adults to take responsibility for making sure students grow socially and emotionally as well as academically. It also requires adults to take full responsibility for their own actions. As Chancellor of the largest school district in the nation, I have taken a stand to support our teachers so they can provide social and emotional learning for the 1.1 million students under their care. A classroom, a school—these communities are built one relationship at a time. When one part, one relationship, in a learning community is harmed or damaged, the wellbeing of the entire community is affected. When we as educators learn more constructive ways to respond to the misbehavior of children, we gain a greater sense of efficacy that extends beyond our instruction and professional identity.

We can do better, but expectation alone is not enough. We need answers and examples like the ones Gianna and Brook provide with great insight from research and practice and great compassion for teachers and students. My hope is that this book will become a touchstone for all of us as we consider social–emotional learning as a path to school reform.

Acknowledgments

The American Standard [bible] translation orders men to triumph over sin. . . . The King James translation makes a promise in "Thou shalt," meaning that men will surely triumph over sin. But the Hebrew word, the word timshel—*"Thou mayest"—that gives a choice. It might be the most important word in the world. That says the way is open. That throws it right back on a man. For if "Thou mayest"—it is also true that "Thou mayest not."*

—JOHN STEINBECK, *East of Eden*

Many years ago I read and reread John Steinbeck's *East of Eden* and the word *timshel* has stayed with me since. It's even led to a tattoo and a child's name. I've thought about this idea of choice so often in my personal life and in my work with children. I've always hoped that through teaching, I could help children recognize that each and every day, we get to choose the kind of person we will be . . . and the kind of person we won't be. This book was born out of the realization that children don't need my hopes, but instead, carefully taught tools that allow them to make that choice.

When I asked my editor if I could include an acknowledgments page in this book, her enthusiastic permission was followed by the question, "How often do you get to make public proclamations of love?" Not nearly often enough. So with that, I have a list of proclamations to make to those who've supported me as I make a daily choice about who I want to be as a person and as an educator, a choice I happily captured on the pages of this book.

The first proclamation of love goes to my editor, Margaret LaRaia, for her consistent encouragement to pursue ideas that are close to my heart and to speak with honesty. Margaret has a gift for giving feedback that is both specific and invitational and a vision for structure that makes even complicated, convoluted ideas seem deliverable. I couldn't have landed in more skilled hands.

Who would have thought that through an arranged writing partnership I might find a soul sister? That's just what happened with Brook Sawyer, my coauthor in both *No More Taking Away Recess and Other Problematic Discipline Practices* (part of the Not This, But That series) and this book. Brook's eternal optimism, razor-sharp readings of my writing, and her own succinct and readable research made coauthorship a joy. I'm not sure I can imagine a book without her.

There have been so many educators I've met along the way who have helped me imagine a better way. But three can't go without mention. My friend and mentor Lucy Malka, whom I met when I was just a wee student teacher and have kept close by ever since, taught me one of the most valuable lessons in life: No matter how good you are at something, you can always be better. Margaret Berry Wilson, whom I met a little bit later, has been a knowledgeable thought partner on the social–emotional learning leg of my journey. She not only helped me imagine a better way but gave me practical strategies to match. Margaret also provided invaluable feedback during the writing of this book. Ellin Keene saw something in me that made her think I could be a writer, and coming from someone as brilliant as she is, that's inspiring encouragement. She is responsible for connecting me to Brook Sawyer and Margaret LaRaia, and for that, I'll be eternally grateful.

I have deep gratitude for my thousand-pound equine teacher, DiMaggio. Whenever I needed a not so gentle reminder (which I needed at multiple points during the writing of this book) of what it is like to be an adult learner, to be out of my comfort zone, to struggle, to fail and try again, to be patient with the learning process, and to pay complete attention, he was sure to provide it. I won't ever forget what I've learned from him.

Someone once told me that if you are an educator and you want to feel appreciated, you should get a dog. So I got three. Obi, Nubie, and Slugger are my most wonderful writing companions. No matter where I am working, they follow, making the writing process not the least bit lonely. And, they always make me feel like I am doing a fantastic job.

Many thanks also to the students, staff, and board at SOAR Charter School at Green Valley Ranch in Denver, Colorado, for graciously allowing me to try out ideas and strategies as I worked on this book and for contributing their own careful thinking.

Finally, the greatest proclamation of love is reserved for my amazing little family. Caleb and Sam give me the most incredible view of child development in action and serve as constant reminders that if something isn't good enough for them (and so much isn't!), then it isn't good enough for any other children. Marc Waxman, my best friend and husband, does everything with kindness and integrity including making sure I have time to write. He encourages me to see the choices I have, to take risks, and to do what feels right even when it isn't easy— both personally and professionally.

To the readers of this book, thank you for doing this work. To say it isn't easy is the greatest of understatements. Remember that there is always a better way, and there is always a choice. *Timshel!*

Gianna Cassetta

Gianna, it is an honor to share a conversation with you, especially one as important as supporting children's social and emotional development. The simultaneous power and vulnerability in your writing inspires me. While reading the drafts of this book, there were times I cheered out loud. You also inspire me in your life. You take risks to live your life with honesty. You indicate that you appreciate my eternal optimism. I am optimistic because I have had the pleasure of knowing so many excellent educators who are constantly reflecting and learning . . . constantly striving to improve education for children, whether that is at the classroom level, the school level, or the field of education level. Margaret, may every writer have the talent, support, and humor that you have offered to Gianna and me.

Brook Sawyer

Introduction

When Things Don't Feel Quite Right, We *Can* Do Better

> *The path of least resistance and least trouble is a mental rut already made.*
> *It requires troublesome work to undertake the alternation of old beliefs.*
>
> —JOHN DEWEY, *Democracy and Education*

Sometimes, in the midst of our teaching, we sense something's not quite right. Despite our diligence and good intentions, our actual instruction and mentorship of children might not quite come together the way we'd imagined. A child misbehaves, and we respond to that misbehavior in a way that doesn't fix the problem. We're not quite clear on how to label what went wrong or what the cause is, but we can feel something's not quite right, and often enough, our students show they feel it, too, so that our classroom or school becomes less of a community and more of a space that individuals simply pass through.

I know that I've had those moments as a teacher and as a principal. On more than one occasion, I've dismissed self-doubt because to respond might mean that I was a failure, or I've chosen frustration instead because I knew I'd done too much that was right to be wrong. It couldn't have been my fault; the fault belongs to someone else. There are certainly times when we have to accept what's beyond our control . . . right?

It's true that we're not omnipotent: we cannot and should not try to control everything that happens. That would be, at the very least, self-defeating behavior and, at the very worst, delusional. *Control* is the wrong word. When we use it or it defines the thinking behind our behavior, we're stuck in the mental rut John Dewey describes. Our job as educators is not to control our students. They can only learn how to behave when they understand why, the decision making and the effects of their behavior. We cannot and should not control our student's behavior, but we are *responsible* for our students and their behavior. To help clarify this distinction, let's consider how health care providers respond when a patient dies, and they wonder if the death could have been prevented. They bring in other staff to examine records of the patient's symptoms at the time of treatment, the diagnosis and treatment of those symptoms, how the patient responded to treatment, and what the patient died of. Although the patient's death is something that cannot be changed, health care providers understand that any negative outcome may hold learning. They hold themselves responsible for considering what they might have done differently. Sometimes an individual health care provider made a choice that could have gone otherwise, sometimes the particulars hold new learning for the field of medicine, and sometimes, despite everyone's best and wise efforts, the patient died. Even when no one is at fault, they are all still responsible.

The field of education does not yet have nationally agreed-upon processes for responding to problems, so, more often than not, we're left to our own devices. Instead of feeling guilt or dismissing our responsibility when our teaching doesn't go well, what if we held onto those moments of self-doubt a little longer, so that we can use them to get better? What if we approached them with curiosity and asked, "Why are you here, and what do you have to teach me?" Let's look at one of my moments of self-doubt together and see what we can gain from this kind of reflection.

"His Behavior Is No Longer Our Problem"

Frankie was one of my most behaviorally challenging students, but in our second year together (I looped with him from fifth to sixth grade) he'd made tremendous growth. When his relationship with the adults at school was strong, Frankie not only held it together but was a sharp, responsible kid with a fantastic sense of humor. But the stresses in Frankie's life were ongoing: his family was poor, his dad was absent from his life for long stretches of time, his mom worked long hours, and he lived in a building with gang members and drug dealers who were eager to "befriend" him.

As teacher and student, we had a strong relationship, but by the time Frankie reached seventh grade, I had stepped out of the classroom to take on school leadership responsibilities. The pressures of neighborhood and home life mounted for Frankie at the same time that he became disconnected from the adults around him. His behavior at school unraveled. He became defiant; he fought a lot; he got "kicked out" of his classroom repeatedly. He didn't trust his teachers; they didn't trust him.

One day, Frankie's antagonistic behavior escalated. My Frankie—the boy who had been a welcome companion on class trips to Chicago and to Bear Lake; who had helped cook dinner in my kitchen; who had become a great student— now held a chair in his hands and was not only swinging it to keep the adults at bay but threatening to use it if they stepped any closer.

In this new and difficult situation, I used the only tool I knew. As the principal, I called Frankie's mom in for a parent conference. If we couldn't get Frankie to comply, she needed to. To communicate the severity of the situation, he was suspended. We told her that when he returned, at any sign of misbehavior, she'd be expected to come in to deal with it. As his mother, his behavior was her responsibility. When I finished, she said to me while holding back tears, "When you are a parent, you'll understand. I'm really disappointed in you, but someday you'll get it."

I was insulted. Hadn't she seen that I'd done everything I could for him, but he'd run out of chances? For the safety of the staff and the other students, we simply could not tolerate his behavior anymore. And as his parent, she had to see that ultimately, this was her responsibility. I didn't need to be a parent to know what was right in this situation. I was a professional, and her child had a problem and she needed to control him. But, even though my colleagues reassured me I had done the right thing, her words unsettled me.

Did I do the right thing? What would you have done if you were in my shoes? Was this an occasion where the responsibility of a school reaches its limits?

For a long time, I didn't know how things worked out for Frankie. His mother pulled him from the school and that was the last I saw of them. But I know now where the path he was on led him. While writing this introduction, I googled his name (changed for this book) and found a newspaper article identifying him both as the perpetrator and the victim of violence.

Maybe you're thinking, "Oh, that's awful, but unfortunately things like that sometimes happen. We do our best, and then we have to move on." I'm not going to counter that statement with an argument for the teacher-as-martyr. That's dangerous and unproductive, often leading teachers to victimize themselves to the unending string of problems we face in today's classrooms. I'm going to say something that feels too often unsaid: Teachers are professionals who make many daily decisions that affect other people's lives, and sometimes, because we are human, we make mistakes. Does that demean our value as professionals? No, you could make the same statement about doctors or the president of our country, but that doesn't mean that they're not competent. Could I have single-handedly eliminated the drug dealers from Frankie's neighborhood, elevated his family's socioeconomic status, and repaired the trauma that made Frankie believe that aggression was an effective solution? While that might make a successful movie, it would hide some essential truths.

Here's the truth that's worth telling. There is no perfect teacher, no perfect school leader, no perfect school. The only "perfect" thing we can do is be willing to revise what we do to make it better. Twenty-two years into teaching and school leadership, I am *still* thinking about the best way to do this work, and I continue to make changes. Over time I have figured out the right questions to ask. My work on answering those questions is ongoing, but I've finally learned enough that's worth sharing, perspectives and tools that can show you how to make classroom management meaningful, achievable, and rewarding.

Instead of teacher martyrdom, let's value hindsight. *Hindsight.* Some of our most important learning comes from looking backward and giving ourselves the space to imagine what we wish had happened. That's the lingering that allows us to begin to dig ourselves out of the mental ruts, so then we can talk, research, and think to identify the tools we need to make that wished-for scenario a reality. In other words, the only way we can become better is to listen to self-doubt. Not to be defeated into paralysis by it, but to use it to identify constructive action. Hindsight affords us a new path and new ways of being, not only for ourselves but for other educators. There aren't enough opportunities for educators to share and learn from each other. I'm hoping this book will create an opportunity for greater dialogue.

If I look back at my story for information that can help us be better for kids like Frankie, their parents, and the educators who work them, I can start to identify what might have been. Frankie's behavior was part of a dialogue between him and his teachers, but did I structure an opportunity for Frankie and his teachers to communicate and give them the tools to move forward? No, instead, I'd stepped in as an authoritarian with a command to fix the situation and provided no clear sense of how to do it. Although I had a good teacher–student relationship with Frankie when he was in my classroom, I didn't have the knowledge or skill to deconstruct my own practice and help teachers do what I'd done. As a principal, I didn't stop him from following the negative momentum created by his behavior; in fact, suspending him reinforced that momentum. Since then, I have done lots of work to make better decisions—ones that are more respectful and more responsive to the information children's misbehavior provides. What should I have done? Well, although there's no single right answer, you'll find plenty of effective alternatives in the pages of this book. And perhaps that is the most important answer at this moment in the book—that too many of us have been following an ineffective, authoritarian model for classroom management and that there are more effective models we can choose. I define *effective* as proven by teachers and academic researchers.

I've written this book because of Frankie, because of children like him all over our country—the children who we try to control, whose very presence screams at us that something isn't right, the ones who beg us to pay attention just a little bit longer so that we can discover a better way to communicate with them. I've written this book because individual hindsight isn't enough if collectively we keep making the same mistakes, having to learn the same lessons. We have to break out of the ruts we are in, even when it is hard, and it is always hard. This book is for all the students who need us to give them the tools and the strategies so they can be successful and happy without being controlled.

REFLECTION   What Troubles Me About My Classroom Management?

Perhaps you're on the same journey. Describe something that troubles you about your classroom management. I'm going to share some examples in teacher language I've heard or used to remind you that you're not alone:

Teachers Talk About Classroom Management Issues

- "I know I'm a good teacher, but there's one student who always puts her head down on her desk through any independent work."

continues

continued

- "In my class this year, I got assigned a group of students who everyone knows come from troubled families and who have real behavioral issues. There's nothing I can do with them, so I focus on the children I can help."
- "He's gotten in several fights this year and administrators do nothing about it. He needs to be suspended."
- "He refuses to stay focused. I have to remind him at least twenty times a day to get back to work."
- "This type of instruction doesn't work for these kids."
- "I can't change how they are; they just have really difficult personalities."
- "My teaching is great when two students are not in the classroom. It isn't acceptable that they're interrupting the other kids' learning, so I send them out of the classroom."
- "My kindergarten student has spit at me several times, and then screams 'no' when I try to send him to the office."
- "In my school we have to give students demerits. So, if a child talks during instruction, you are supposed to give him or her a demerit. Even if it is over something benign, like, a kid drops his pen or pencil and whispers, 'Could you get that pencil for me?' or 'Thank you' after someone picks it up. You will definitely get spoken to by an administrator if you are caught not using the demerit system, so I just follow the procedure even though I think it is wrong."

Did any of these resonate with you? To better understand this issue, use the questions that follow to describe it with specific, objective details.

Identifying a Problem

- When did this happen? (If recurrent, describe one specific occasion.)
- What were the triggers? What seemed to be the cause(s) of the behavior?
- What did you feel?
- How did you respond?

How did the event resolve itself, or is it ongoing? If ongoing, does the behavior happen under the same conditions? If so, what are they?

Right now, you're researching yourself as an educator. Like any great researcher, you're recording as much objective data as you can, first. This book will help you interpret the behavior and help you choose an effective response. We'll focus on moving from blame (of yourself, your students, and/or others) onto constructive action, and we'll do so by addressing questions central both to effective classroom management and effective teaching (because one can't really happen without the other).

- Who Am I? Who Are My Students? (Chapter 1)
- What Do I Want for My Students? (Chapter 2)
- How Do I Set Boundaries and Teach Expectations? (Chapter 3)
- Why Do Children Misbehave and How Should I Respond? (Chapter 4)
- How Can Instruction Help Students Practice and Reflect on Behavior? (Chapter 5)

There's always learning to do, which is another way of saying that making mistakes is inevitable. Let's learn from our mistakes together.

1

WHO AM I? WHO ARE MY STUDENTS?

The highest form of love is the love that allows for intimacy without the annihilation of difference.

—PARKER J. PALMER, *The Courage to Teach:*
Exploring the Inner Landscape of a Teacher's Life

When you close your eyes and call up the image of a teacher, who do you see? Who teaches in the United States of America? A majority of teachers nationally are white—white middle-class females.

Maybe you are, too. And maybe you are wondering how that could possibly matter. If you've been trained for the profession, if you know your craft, and if you care about your students, why should race or gender or socioeconomic status matter in how you teach or how you manage classrooms? Before answering that difficult question, I want you to know that I too am a white female educator.

It has taken a long time, a long and hard time, to accept that my identity matters. I had the unique experience of growing up in a neighborhood in NYC where I was the minority—the only white student in most of my K–8 years at a school in East Harlem. Although I knew that I was "different," it wasn't until I went to an elite all-girls, mostly white high school that I became acutely aware that racism existed. I became acutely aware that my experience living and learning with children of color was painfully different from how my white wealthy classmates perceived them. My entry into teaching was motivated by my desire to contribute to an equitable and just education system for children who I knew have systematically been denied access to high-quality, fair opportunities in schools. I was a trained teacher, I was a student of the craft, and I adored my students. Whenever I was in a meeting where the question was asked, "Why don't these teachers look more like our students?" I believed it was a petty question to be asking, and so, over and over again, I dismissed it.

It really wasn't until I became a school leader in Harlem that I paid attention. Maybe it was the experience of stepping out of my classroom, and having a larger worldview that allowed me to do that. Over and over again, families saw me as another white woman coming into their neighborhood to impose my values on their children, and when you hear something enough times, you have a duty to stop being dismissive and try to hear what is really being said. Race and socioeconomic status simply can't be ignored.

But I don't want you to just take my word for it. Reading one source on classroom management can miscommunicate the idea that all the wisdom on classroom management can/should be contained in one source. If this book were told only from the perspective of my anecdotal experience as an educator, you'd be right to question it. You've heard that expression "No man is an island," and yet all too often a solitary teacher is expected to have all the answers. Instead, we need to reach beyond ourselves for answers—discuss important topics with colleagues, read what smart people in the field have to say—and then synthesize that information within the context of our own experience. Because I believe that this kind of collaboration is essential, this book models it. At key moments throughout the book, you'll find context from research provided by Brook Sawyer, a professor in education. When I pose a question, it's not a rhetorical tool, but a reminder that even though we are not in the same room, this book is a conversation among you, Brook, and me. So, instead of me only reporting my experience, let's look at what the research tells us about teacher and student identity.

Teacher and Student Demographics

According to the National Center for Education Statistics (NCES)[1] (2013), public school teachers are mainly white (82 percent). Females dominate the profession (74 percent), particularly in the elementary grades (89 percent). The average

---

1. The figures represent the most recent data that were publicly available during the writing of this book.

teaching salary in 2011–2012 school year was approximately $53,000, indicative of a middle socioeconomic salary.

The demographics of the student body are much more diverse than the teaching staff. In fall 2014, approximately 50 million students attended public school (NCES 2014). Nationally, white students make up about 50 percent of the student population, with that percentage expected to decline to approximately 45 percent over the next decade. Black students constitute approximately 15 percent of the student population. Hispanic students make up approximately 25 percent of the student population. The Hispanic student population is growing dramatically; by 2023, the Hispanic student population is projected to be 30 percent. These statistics certainly vary by region. For example, the West has the highest percentage of Hispanic students (41 percent), whereas the Midwest has a lower Hispanic student population (11 percent).

Additionally, the eligibility of students for free and reduced price lunch (FRPL), which is an indication of poverty, is growing (NCES 2013). In the 2011–2012 school year, 47 percent of students attended schools that were characterized as mid-high or high poverty, whereas this was the case for 28 percent of students in 1999–2000 school year. A high-poverty school has 75 percent or more of students receiving FRPL, and a midpoverty school has 50–74 percent of students receiving FRPL.

Understanding Our Responses to Race and Gender

The statistics that Brook shared reflect my experience. The schools I have taught in and led in have comprised an overwhelmingly white female staff and a student body made up mostly of students of color. It has been my experience, time and time again, that relationships between *many* staff and students are tenuous. There are too many children who teachers don't know well and don't like. The students are resistant, and instead of drawing them in, the teachers build parallel walls. I have to believe that the root cause is racial, socioeconomic, and gender imbalance. In other words, the root cause is difference.

The reality is that as far as we have come in our country around issues of race and gender, we really haven't come that far, and honest, reflective dialogue about race and gender remains sensitive, uncomfortable, and for the most part, something to be avoided. The truth is that differences—all kinds of differences—make us uncomfortable *at best*. At worst, differences stir feelings so deep that they drive some to feel justified in violence.

How many times have you passed and quickly looked away from someone who *looks* different to seem as if you didn't notice or didn't care—the burn victim, the person with the large birthmark on his face, the child with the chromosomal disorder? How many times have you or someone you know reacted with discomfort toward belief- or value-based differences? "They are or believe [fill-in-the-blank], so I can't talk to them." We all create boundaries that define those who are different from us. Although that defining of difference is a normal part of identity, it is destructive when the difference becomes a barrier that prevents us from knowing the other. Too often that barrier allows us to make simplistic and destructive judgments. How many times have you said or heard comments in schools that imply a judgment has been made about students or families being different? Here are some I've heard, and continue to hear:

- "Those kids don't learn that way."
- "These kids need structure and consequences."
- "She thinks it's okay to do that here because that's what she sees at home."
- "Those parents don't care and are no help."
- "Of course he didn't take responsibility . . . boys from that culture get babied."

Notice there's no *I* in the statements I just listed. Reactions to differences, whether ones of judgment or discomfort, occur for most of us multiple times a day, but we are socialized to pretend they are not real—someone else has issues, but we don't. But they are real. We all have those reactions—all of us. And often we have them in our schools and in our classrooms.

What's really going on for us when we have these reactions? How do these reactions impact our ability to work effectively with children? How can they get in the way of us striking a balance between intimate, productive relationships and confident leadership in classroom management?

Color-Blindness

Color-blind is a sociological term that refers to the ability to ignore race, because racism is no longer a discriminating factor. I have heard so many teachers (who look a whole lot like me) say that "it doesn't matter" what their students look like.

In fact, they "don't even notice." Racism is still a blatant problem in the United States. To deny its existence is to deny reality. It becomes impossible to establish trust with others if we can't acknowledge who they are, what they need, and what experiences they bring to the classroom with them.

White Guilt

White guilt is the other side of the color-blind coin. It is the individual or collective guilt often said to be felt by some white people for the racist treatment of people of color by whites both historically and presently. I have worked with numerous staff who could not appropriately or safely establish authority, because "they felt bad for" the students.

Lack of Perspective

Simply put, when staff lack diversity, they lack the ability to look at issues (or students) through a variety of lenses and experiences, which leads to low capacity for problem solving and change. A friend told me about her consulting experience in a white public school, where she was there to talk about issues of equity and social justice. "We don't want our kids to know about that here," a teacher told her, "We don't even have those kinds of kids in our community."

Fear

I believe much of our discomfort with difference comes from fear. Racism is still a blatant problem in the United States. It is fueled by fear of what is different, fear of the unknown. Particularly as students get older, it becomes more common to hear teachers say, "I'm scared of those kids." Would they jokingly say such a thing if those children looked like their own sons and daughters, nieces or nephews? Probably not. Let's dip back into the research to consider what this means for the teacher–student relationship.

Teacher–Student Relationships

Ethnic minority and students who live in poverty are more likely to face risk factors, such as familial instability, harsh parenting, and exposure to violence, which impact their behavior in the classroom (Oshima et al. 2010). Not surprisingly when we consider these risk factors, students who live in poverty underperform academically when compared to their white, middle-class peers (Hoff 2013).

A critical way to improve the outcomes of students, particularly our vulnerable youth, is to develop positive teacher–student relationships. This is because relationships are a way to meet students' needs of relatedness, competence, and autonomy. A close relationship with a teacher provides a child with a feeling of relatedness. In turn, this secure relationship allows him or her to safely explore and engage in challenging learning tasks, which thereby improve children's competency and autonomy (Birch and Ladd 1997; Pianta 1999). Students, including those with diagnosed behavior disorders, report that their most effective teachers established caring relationships with them (Woolfolk-Hoy and Weinstein 2006). When students are part of positive teacher–student relationships and overall caring classrooms communities, they do better socially and academically (e.g., Patrick et al. 2003; Roorda et al. 2011; Watson and Battistich 2006).

As we know, relationships involve two people. The transactional theory describes how one person's (even a child's) actions influence our behavior toward that person (Sameroff and Fiese 2000). As a simple example of this theory: It is easier to be kind to a person when he or she treats you kindly. For teachers, student behavior and characteristics influence the relationships you form with them. Researchers have found that teachers develop closer relationships with students who are more mature and intelligent (Ladd, Birch, and Buhs 1999; Mantzicopoulos 2005). Conversely, they develop more distant or conflictual relationships with children who display problem behaviors, such as anger and hyperactivity (Justice et al. 2008; Ladd, Birch, and Buhs 1999; Mantzicopoulos 2005; Thijs and Koomen 2009).

Typically, girls have more positive teacher–student relationships than boys (Birch and Ladd 1997; Hamre and Pianta 2001; O'Connor and McCartney 2006). This makes sense given that boys may be more physically active, impulsive, dysregulated, and faster to frustrate and anger than girls (Else-Quest et al. 2006; Zahn-Waxler, Shiftcliff, and Marceau 2008). Also, children who are ethnic minority and poor also are more likely to share negative relationships with their teachers than children who are white and higher socioeconomic status (Ladd, Birch, and Buhs 1999; O'Connor and McCartney 2006).

In addition to knowing that your relationships with students impact their performance, it is very important to note that the relationships you form with students are predicative of the students' subsequent relationships with teachers (e.g., Hamre and Pianta 2001; Hughes et al. 2008; Wu, Hughes, and Kwok 2010). That is, if students have more positive relationships with their early elementary teachers, they are more likely to have positive relationships with their later elementary and secondary teachers. The reverse is also true. When students have negative relationships with their early elementary teachers, they are more likely to continue this less than optimal type of relationship with their later elementary and secondary teachers.

REFLECTION   What Do I Know About My Students?

This is not meant to be a series of accusations against who teachers happen to be as people. It's an opportunity to check in with yourself and your colleagues about what is happening at your school. It is an invitation to heighten awareness of those feelings of discomfort, to catch ourselves, question ourselves, and, ultimately, choose our actions with greater care and wisdom. We can't change the face of the teaching population overnight, but we can get to the highest form of love for our students, where we not only tolerate but take delight in their differences from ourselves and each other. And that starts with an approach to building relationships.

Trusting intimate relationships with children is a challenging issue in many schools. Oftentimes we trivialize or underestimate what it means to develop authentic relationships with children. In one school I worked at, I enlisted the help of a trusted friend and colleague of mine, Margaret Berry-Wilson, who has written extensively about social and emotional learning in books such as *The Language of Learning* (2014) and *Teasing, Tattling, Defiance and More* (2013). In a session focused on the teacher–student relationships, she nailed it with this task: Make a list of all the students in your class. Write down five personal pieces of information you know about each student you teach. In other words, not just whether or not Johnny comes to school on time or is good at math, but whether or not Johnny has a dog or a baby sister or likes the Red Sox or the Yankees. Because, of course, when you have good relationships with people, you know lots about them. And then came the *eews* of discomfort and the *ohs* of realization. There were too many children who teachers just did not know *anything* about. Try it yourself. Examine your relationship with your students.

continues

continued

Examine the Teacher–Student Relationship: Know Who Your Students Are

What do I know about my students?

Choose one student you find difficult. Write down five personal pieces of information you know about that one student.

If you don't know who your students are, you can't teach them. That's not just my opinion. Here are three thinkers across the span of more than 250 years who believe the same:

- "You only learn from those you love."—Johann Wolfgang von Goethe, eighteenth-century German writer and politician
- "No significant learning occurs without a significant relationship."—James Comer, professor of child psychiatry, 1995
- "Children learn best when they like their teacher and think their teacher likes them."— Gordon Neufeld, developmental psychologist, *Hold On to Your Kids: Why Parents Need to Matter More Than Peers*

This isn't new insight, but it's not emphasized enough. Through trusting relationships with adults—ones *characterized by teachers and children enjoying being together, with teachers knowing children well, providing assistance (emotionally and instructionally) when needed, and displaying a warm and responsive demeanor to students*—children learn that others can be responsive to their needs. Trusting relationships allow for achievable and safe learning experiences where children practice communicating, facing challenges, and experiencing and regulating emotions. Positive, supportive relationships with children help them develop socially and emotionally and enable you to effectively manage your classroom. Children spend an average of thirty-five hours a week, ten months out of the year, with school-based adults—so positive relationships with teachers and school staff are critical for healthy development.

The closeness of a relationship is defined not only by what we know about each other but also by how we respond to one another. So, let's return to that difficult student and look at our interaction.

Examine the Teacher–Student Relationship: Evaluate How You Interact

Identify whether each of the following statements accurately describes your interaction with a challenging student.

- When redirected, this student adjusts and moves on.
- I know where I stand with this student—our interactions are generally positive, predictable, and consistent.
- The student shares personal updates and feelings with me without much prompting.
- I share laughs with this student.
- This student seeks help from me when necessary.
- I enjoy my interactions with this student.
- I can easily name several positive qualities about this student.

How to Build More Positive Teacher–Student Relationships

If you disagreed with any of these statements while considering a particular student, it might be necessary to put time into building a more positive relationship. Let's explore some practical ways to build relationships with students.

Learn About Your Students' Lives Outside of School

Early in the school year, one way to accomplish this is through a beginning-of-year family interview. Never underestimate what families can and will share, regardless of their socioeconomic or cultural background. Families love to tell you all the great, quirky things about the children they live with and love. Collecting interview information, either by phone, in person, or in writing, is an easy way to learn lots about children. If you need a translator, get one, but ask families to tell you about their children. Here is an example of a really simple survey and the feedback provided by a parent (Figure 1–1).

Family Survey

Student Name: **Sam**

1. Tell me about pets/siblings/family members:

   You've met Sam's big bro, Davis. Sam loves being around and playing with Davis, but they bicker all the time, never about anything important, and they always make up five minutes later. He plays lots of sports with Davis and his Dad—which I try and stay out of. I'm Sam's comfort object. He likes time alone with me to snuggle, read, or watch movies. We have dogs, and Sam likes to "get low" with them, roll around with them, let them slobber on him, etc.

2. What does your child love about school?

   Choice is definitely the favorite time of his day, but Sam likes school so on any given day he might speak very positively about any subject. He adores his friends—Allen, Marcus, and Pedro. He talks about them all the time and says they always look out for each other.

3. Does your child have any struggles outside of school that would be helpful to know about?

   Sam and Davis have two brothers the same age who they are best friends with. But even so, Sam acts the "youngest" and can get left out. He argues a lot, he will actually look for things to argue about. Whereas Davis gets mad during sports if you don't follow the rules correctly, Sam will argue to change a rule because it is stupid. He might even go so far as to argue that a flower that is red is really lavender, that something is wrong with your eyes for seeing red. It can be funny at times and at other times completely frustrating. And I know sometimes, these kinds of issues can come up in the classroom.

4. Other important things to know about your child:

   Sam is such a loving kid, super in touch with his emotions. Best darn hugger on earth. He loves highly physical play (you should see him throw his body around the basketball court), but also quiet play like stringing necklaces. When he gets interested in a subject he wants to know everything about it. For example, if he hears something about gladiators, he wants to learn all about them, read different books and stories about them, watch videos about them, go to Rome and see where they fought. He likes catching and observing bugs. He has no fear, isn't squeamish, will let things crawl all over him. He has a great, great sense of humor. Did I mention he has the best hugs on earth?

Figure 1–1. Family Survey

Use What You Learn About Students to Grow a Connection

I remember meeting someone in high school who has since become a lifelong friend. She still teases me about my inability to make small talk—she tried multiple times across our science lab tables to get a conversation going. But when she saw me drawing the name of one of my favorite bands in block letters across my notebook, she had an "in." She used something she learned about me to start a conversation—the first one that went successfully, and from there it was history!

You can use the interview similarly. Four simple questions, and look at the amazing information! Sam's teacher now has an immediate in to a relationship with Sam. Once you learn about a child, you must use the information to let students know you have noticed them, they are significant, and you want to know more. For example, ask:

- "How are the dogs, Sam?"
- "Did you play any sports this weekend with your dad and Davis?"
- "Sam, would you like to take a magnifying glass out to recess today to observe insects?"
- "I heard you have a great sense of humor. . . . I have a joke for you. Knock knock. . . . "
- "Sam, I know what good friends you are with Allen, Marcus, and Pedro and that you all take really good care of each other. Can you four help me by being responsible for taking out and bringing in all the recess equipment this week?"

Show Children That You Will Keep Them Safe

There are few things more detrimental to any student–teacher relationship than for the child to believe the adult is not looking out for their emotional or physical well-being. Children watch us and they notice if we care if they are being treated well, unfairly, or inappropriately. They see it when we overlook or ignore mistreatment, and they can become downright and justly outraged. How many times have your students come back from being with another teacher fuming that another student misbehaved toward them and that the teacher "did nothing"? Let students know that you expect everyone in your class to be treated with kindness, and mean it.

Never ignore hurtful remarks children make to each other. Remarks like "Stupid," "Here comes fatty," or "Your hair smells" are hurtful and simply can't go ignored. A simple response is to hold eye contact and say, "We use kind words in our classroom. Try that again." Students will only have trusting relationships with adults who look out for their emotional and physical well-being.

Remember to always "close the loop" with children. If you saw something, or if they came to you crying, let them know you are aware and that you will take action. When action has been taken, whether big or small, check in again, so that they don't think you "did nothing."

Show Students Who Are Having a Hard Time That You Care and Are Available

The school day is too busy for lots of one-on-one time, and yet, fifteen minutes a week before or after school to check in with a student who is struggling can go such a long way toward establishing a strong relationship. It might even be the first fifteen minutes of every prep period, with you and your student chatting while you make photocopies. When students are struggling, adults in schools can provide an important resource by being the person students can talk to about a difficult issue. It is incredibly meaningful to a student just to be listened to, fully and sincerely, even when they are in the wrong.

As well, you can be a helper during the school day. It is okay to say to a student, "If you have trouble getting started, raise your hand to let me know—I want to help you."

Look carefully at your students and identify one or two you can try this with. Make a regular schedule for check-ins and put them on your calendar. You and your student will grow to understand each other in ways that would never occur in a whole-class setting. The important thing is to be consistent—only set up check-ins if you are committed to following through; otherwise this can cause greater distance in the relationship.

Spend Nontraditional Academic Time or Nonacademic Time with Students

If you really want to build a relationship with a student, you may need to show up for them in the same way you expect them to show up in your class. When you plan that next field trip, be sure the students who you need to bond with are in your group. Don't put them with the parent volunteer. If you have a child who misbehaves in your class but is stellar in art, go visit him in art class and sit next to him, ask what he is thinking and doing. Imagine ways he can do similar work in your class. Eat lunch with your students, and be very intentional about who you eat with, and how often. Play with your students at recess—not just the students who are easy to play with but also the ones who are not. Ask them to teach you their favorite recess game. Invite children to come in early for breakfast or plan a movie and popcorn night. These efforts aren't a reward for good student behavior and should not be withheld because of misbehavior. These are strategies for building good relationships.

Validate Their Feelings

Feelings aren't wrong, even if you don't share them. When you have the student who comes back from recess and her behavior is escalating, yelling that she got pushed and is going to punch someone in the face, try empathizing out loud by giving her a mirror to her feelings. "Gosh! Demaris, that is so upsetting that you got pushed on the playground! Tell me what happened, I need to hear this!" By showing empathy and being a good listener, you'll make students more open to your advice on what to do next. This kind of interaction shows children "I get you."

Speak with Positivity and Compassion

No one likes people who criticize them all the time. As my colleague Margaret has wisely said, teaching is the one job where you have to find something to like about all of your students. Find it, and tell them. Everyone has competencies even if they aren't the ones you want them to have. When a child who has been hitting picks up supplies that dropped to the floor, tell them what good care they are talking of materials. Remember to communicate with compassion and kindness especially when you are most frustrated with a student.

A positive relationship does not mean an easy one. Intimacy is the result of commitment and work. If you think about any positive long-term relationship you have had—with a sibling, a teacher, a parent, a friend, a coworker, or a partner— you can identify unavoidable difficulties. What defines the quality of the relationship isn't just your ability to get along but your commitment to figuring things out when you don't. When a student knows that you still see her value even when she doesn't hand in her research project, that student is more likely to come to you and figure out how she can complete her work *even though* she is overwhelmed. When a student believes you know he's more than the bad decision that made him shove another child off the monkey bars, he is more receptive to taking responsibility for his behavior *even though* he can't yet imagine how to behave differently. Positive relationships remind us that we don't have to be perfect. A positive relationship is a bridge that helps us over difficulty. Too often in teaching and in American culture, we deny that difficulty is inevitable—the teacher-as-martyr, the myth of the individual, the cult of perpetual happiness—all these narratives lead us away from the truth that life can be hard and that every human being is flawed. To the degree that we don't acknowledge this in our teaching and in our relationships with our students, we set them up for the shame and guilt that traps them in negative behavior. Take a moment to describe your most positive relationship. One shared trait of all positive relationships is that the other person helps us imagine and become a better version of ourselves. That also defines our responsibility as educators. Your students need you to commit to a positive relationship with them.

2

What Do I Want for My Students?

> *One's philosophy is not best expressed in words; it is expressed in the choices one makes . . . and the choices we make are ultimately our responsibility.*
>
> —ELEANOR ROOSEVELT, *You Learn by Living: Eleven Keys for a More Fulfilling Life*

If you asked most of us in our best moments what we want our classroom management practices to teach children, our responses would be grand. We do this work because of our devotion to children. We believe that every child can develop into a joyful and successful adult, and we want to know that our work is helping to make that happen. But all too often we get overwhelmed. In that state of being overwhelmed, the likelihood that we will make a poor decision becomes high—especially when it comes to classroom management. To avoid the pull of that bad momentum, we need to be anchored by understandings and practices, so that even in the most difficult times, we can act in ways that redirect misbehaving students onto a more positive path.

Recently, I was hired as a consultant to coach for a week in a fairly new teacher's classroom. My job was to model literacy practices for teachers in the school. On that first day, I arrived in the classroom thirty minutes early to observe the class' morning routines and meeting before I was scheduled to teach. As the teacher explained her instruction, several students ignored her to focus on an insult-hurling competition: "You stupid"; "Duh"; "Why don't you shut up?" Each tried to one-up the others by silencing them through humiliation. Other students talked to each other civilly while ignoring the teacher. She kept trying to redirect them with ever so gentle commands (sometimes so quiet I wasn't sure she had said something) that were ignored or argued with. The toxic mix of disrespect, animosity, and disorder meant that teaching literacy couldn't yet be the agenda. I had to address this teacher's classroom management practices.

To be frank, I wasn't calm about this situation. The next day, I was supposed to be modeling literacy practices for a group of visiting teachers in this classroom. Why hadn't the administrators or teachers warned me? Although I am very confident in my ability to manage a classroom, reversing the culture of a classroom in a few minutes is difficult, if not impossible. Kids were going to show up to class the next day with an expectation of chaos and disrespect. Some of them would work hard to maintain that momentum, and I would have to spend my energy on redirecting that, in addition to modeling exemplary literacy practices. By two minutes into my first lesson, I knew for certain that there wasn't enough of a preexisting positive classroom environment for me to demonstrate good teaching and learning. It was a disaster. I pushed through that one lesson as best as I could and decided to use what I saw to figure out an action plan moving forward. I could easily have gone into a deficit mode and illustrated everything that was wrong with what the teacher had been doing, but because I was hired as a consultant and because of how I choose to live in the world, I focused on working from where we were.

So where were we? Like so many fourth graders, this group of students were in that challenging yet delicate developmental phase where they can be so critical of themselves, and even more so of others. They need teachers to build strong communities with clear boundaries to keep them safe and strong. But what they had were "soft limits." A caring teacher who had rules but didn't enforce them. A community in which they could frequently insult each other without an adult making it stop. The teacher didn't understand what her instruction was communicating. She thought if she enforced rules, if she silenced their criticism, they would think she didn't like them, and in turn, they wouldn't like her. So, my plan of action focused on establishing a better learning environment with literacy practices as the vehicle for those classroom management moves. I wanted to show her that part of caring about students is making sure they don't hurt each other physically or emotionally. I needed her to see that children respond to the boundaries that keep them safe with reciprocal caring.

The very next day, when I taught the class again, I was told that day I had created "a different class." I'll name a few key things I did in between the first and second lessons, but know that I'll be talking about these all in greater depth throughout the book.

1. **Prioritized relationships with the most challenging students.** Between lessons I met with the ten most boisterous students individually. I tried to get to know a little bit about them. I asked them how they felt about the way they and their classmates treated each other, and how they could imagine that being different and more positive. I also shared what I saw, why it wasn't productive, and what I expected to be different. I told them I'd be speaking to the whole class. This was time-consuming, but you can't positively manage a challenging class you aren't connected with.

2. **Shared goals and purposes of our work with the whole class.** I met with the class as a whole briefly—I was very authoritative, but positive. I told them I was there to teach them the skills they needed to be more collaborative, creative, independent, and productive (and yes, I used adult language on purpose and treated them like I believed they were sophisticated, which they were!). I let them know that I would be very clear and direct with them about how to do that but when I gave a direction, I expected the directions to be followed. I told them I'd give them lots of feedback on how they were doing, which I did at every opportunity.

3. **Provided students opportunity and choice to practice.** Students needed to understand that this was their time. I involved them in the lessons as much as I could—with as little teacher talk and as much student talk as possible and choices whenever possible.

I have the tools and confidence now to be my best self with students most of the time. Just like your students are works in progress, I wasn't always this way. Too often, teachers think they can turn around a "bad" class through one good lesson or one conversation with a challenging student. No doubt these individual actions do make a difference, and sometimes it's a giant leap forward, but what really matters is how those daily actions accumulate over time into expectations for how we behave and how we respond to each other when there are problems. Students will disrupt, and that's not necessarily a bad thing. We do want them to challenge us when what we're doing something that doesn't make sense to them.

When we expect that student misbehavior will happen, when we expect that some students might have difficulty sometimes, then we are in a stance of thoughtful readiness. When we expect that all students will behave the way we want all the time, well, that's just not the way the world works.

REFLECTION What Behavior Do I Expect from Other Adults?

A wise, mature person expects both good *and* bad behavior from the adults she interacts with every day. It's worth staying with this idea for a moment because realistic expectations are essential to this work. When individuals are held to high expectations that are not tempered by reality, they often feel resentful and angry at the person measuring them by those high expectations and/or they feel low self-esteem because they cannot meet the expectations. In turn, the person holding the high expectations is surprised and disappointed by those who can't meet them. The outcome is estrangement. Nothing changes and nothing new can be communicated. Has this ever happened in a relationship of yours?

So, for example, if you expect your coworker not to gossip casually about someone else's marital problems but she does it, when you show her your displeasure, what are you accomplishing? She thinks you're a jerk; you think she's a jerk. And that's where you will both stay.

What if instead of judging her for gossiping, you confronted your colleague in a way that would allow you to stay true to yourself, allow her to understand your perspective, and give her the opportunity to leave the conversation as a better person? What if you said something like, "Gosh, I've always really liked working with you. You've been such a good colleague. And so has Dolores. So I was just taken by surprise when I heard you talking about her marital problems in the staff room. I just didn't expect that. And because I care about you both I just had to tell you how uncomfortable that was for me." I don't know about you, but if someone called me out with such kindness and care, I don't know how I could think of her as a jerk. And, I don't know how it couldn't heighten my awareness of my public behavior. I'd feel like I was invited to the possibility of being a better person than I was in an earlier moment in time.

continues

continued

Identify Ideal and Expected Behaviors

Think about at least one ongoing difficult relationship you have. What are the behaviors of that person that make you frustrated/disappointed? List them out. What do you wish for instead? You should have a list of ideal and expected behaviors.

If you're open to doing so, it might be worthwhile to consider what you do to maintain the negative momentum in this relationship. Every relationship is transactional. You might not be able to change this person through your behavior, but I'm guessing there's something you can identify that you wish you could do but can't yet. List those ideal and expected behaviors as well.

We have to be prepared for ideal and expected behaviors. Our contemporary culture allows us to insulate ourselves, and new teachers are often unprepared for bad behavior. In our adult lives, we self-select by choosing friends, professions, and partners to create a community of people who are agreeable to us. Although we do encounter difficulties—an argument with a partner, a coworker we can't relate to—much of our exposure to people we might have difficulty with can be controlled. That degree of control can create an unrealistic expectation of agreement. We don't choose the individuals who come into our classroom. There will be personalities in your classroom who are antithetical to your own. But guess what? Learning how to connect to those students, despite the differences, is the growing required of teaching. It's the growing you want of your students, too. You don't want them to miss an opportunity because they can't get along with a certain type of person. Instead, you want them to learn how to respond to difficult personalities and situations in a way that keeps positive possibility open.

What we want, both for ourselves and for our students, is efficacy. *Efficacy* is the capacity or power to reach a desired effect or outcome. Efficacy breeds efficacy. Imagine all the actions you take in a day, from the mundane to the magnificent—from styling your hair to that perfect curl to helping a child learn a new skill or change behavior. This might also be the day you convince your supermarket manager to carry a healthier product, your principal to make a schedule change, a donor to fund a project. The more you recognize your capacity to get the results you want, the more you are willing to try out that power in new situations.

The same is true with children—they too learn efficacy through experience. As adults, we must set up the experiences for them to ensure that the experience is possible. In school, these experiences might take the form of:

- a child having a fellow classmate stop his pencil tapping by explaining that the sound is distracting
- choosing a group of peers to sit with and work with to study a research topic they have selected together
- a set of children being responsible for setting up, collecting, and emptying recycling bins throughout the school
- students deciding they are going to study and educate others about the plight of homelessness and organizing a food and clothing drive for a local shelter.

Students with strong social skills and a sense of efficacy can easily be taught to have a critical mind. They can evaluate the world they live in. They can identify issues, ask questions, and test out answers. They can plan for and advocate for improvements. Is there anyone who wouldn't want a child to develop these skills? Can you imagine a society in which schools no longer imposed classroom management systems to control children but utilized ones that teach social and emotional competence, efficacy, and action? I have seen it happen on a small scale, in specific classrooms and schools, and I believe it can and must happen for all teachers and children. In the next section, Brook will explain the research-based goals we should be reaching for.

Social–Emotional Competencies

What does the research recommend for our goals for student behavior? Researchers use the term *social–emotional competencies*, and they've identified five categories (Payton et al. 2008):

1. Students should be *self-aware*, which means students are cognizant of their own emotions.

2. They should be able to *self-manage*, which includes impulse control, appropriate display of emotions, and goal-setting.
3. They should be *socially aware*, meaning that they are able to engage in perspective-taking and modify their own actions in accordance with the at-hand situation.
4. They also should demonstrate *positive relationship skills* to develop meaningful relationships with peers as well as teachers and other adults.
5. They should exhibit *responsible decision making*, including decisions about safety, treating others respectfully, and learning.

It is important to recognize that these skills are intertwined. For instance, Micah is playing kickball at recess. When his kick is caught and he is called "out," he recognizes he feels disappointed (*self-aware*). Yet, despite his disappointment, he cheers on the next player at bat, saying, "You can do it!" In this way, he made a *responsible decision* to manage his behavior (*self-management*) so that he was a good teammate (*social awareness* and *positive relationship skills*).

As another example, consider Destiny, who is working in a small group. Her teacher has told each group of students to select an animal to research for their marine biology project. Two students in her group are arguing about whether to pick the sea lion or the walrus. Personally, Destiny wants to study the sea lion but knows that a good way to solve the problem is for each student to vote, rather than having everyone continue to argue about their group's selection. Thus, she inhibits her own preference (*self-awareness* and *self-management*) to suggest what is best for the group (*social awareness, responsible decision making,* and *positive relationship skills*). The group votes for the sea lion. Destiny is happy (*self-awareness*) but knows that her friend in her group who wanted the walrus feels sad (*social awareness*) so she does not gloat. Instead, she makes a *responsible decision* that works to *build positive relationships* by telling her friend that she can choose how they will report their work to the whole class (e.g., poster board, PowerPoint presentation, etc.).

As expected, students who are more socially and emotionally competent are "better behaved" (i.e., exhibit more positive behaviors) in the classroom (Blum and Libbey 2004; Greenberg et al. 2003). Furthermore, these social and emotional skills translate into the academic domain. A robust amount of research indicates that children who are socially and emotionally competent demonstrate self-control, attention, and persistence in completing tasks, which lead to better academic performance (e.g., Coolahan et al. 2000; Graziano et al. 2007; Hughes et al. 2008; Klem and Connell 2004; Normandeau and Guay 1998; Wentzel 1993). These markers of success are not just short term: Students who have better social and emotional competence are more likely to graduate high school and have better employment opportunities (Blum and Libbey 2004; Greenberg et al. 2003).

The great news for us as teachers is that teaching these skills makes a difference: Students show better behavior and more positive attitudes when teachers explicitly teach students social–emotional skills (Durlak et al. 2011). First and foremost, teachers need to build an inclusive and welcoming classroom community. When children feel they belong to a community, they behave better because they want their community to remain a positive place (Patrick et al. 2003; Solomon et al. 2000). The development of caring relationships between and among teachers and students is imperative. Teachers should demonstrate a positive and supportive demeanor with students, show students they are glad to see them by greeting them, take the time to know their students as people, and actively listen to students (Bohn, Roehrig, and Pressley 2004; Fallon, O'Keeffe, and Sugai 2012). Second, just like academic skills, behavioral skills can be taught with the gradual release of responsibility model: modeling, guided practice, and independent practice (Gettinger and Kohler 2006). Specific practices will be described in Chapter 5.

A hallmark of effective approaches to support students' social–emotional learning is that they have a broader focus than just what is happening in the individual classroom (CASEL 2014; Lochman, Salekin, and Haaga 2003). That is, effective social–emotional learning (SEL) programs target children's learning across a variety of settings: classroom, schoolwide, and at home. In this way, children have consistent support and expectations for practicing SEL skills. For a helpful resource of different SEL programs and their evidence of effectiveness, see www. casel.org/guide/ratings/elementary (CASEL 2014).

How Should Child Development Inform Our Expectations?

Whenever we are thinking about teaching children SEL competencies, there is always the question of development to consider. What does it mean for a five-year-old to self-manage as opposed to a ten-year-old? How does our own awareness of ourselves develop over time? What should it look like in second grade, or in sixth? So many times, we think children are misbehaving, when really what they are doing is "being six" or "being eleven." How many fifth-grade teachers out there have become exasperated at how argumentative their students are, when really, those fifth graders are developing a sense of what is right and wrong and figuring out how to establish boundaries?

I remember my first year with seventh graders. I'd always had such positive rewarding experiences with students up through sixth grade, but this year, I could do no right in the eyes of the seventh graders. They complained constantly that I "didn't understand" and that "no one listens to them." I thought all I had been doing was listening, and all they had been doing was complaining. It wasn't until a brilliant colleague of mine visited and said, "That's seventh grade—that's developmental. You need to have a lot of empathy for seventh graders. Here's what's going on and here's what you do. . . . "

Knowing what is developmentally appropriate is incredibly useful in terms of managing a classroom and making decisions about how to support students in terms of SEL competencies. But it is also incredibly imperfect. First, our sense of what is right and wrong develops and changes over a lifetime and is impacted by numerous factors. Not only is each individual unique in terms of development, but development may be impacted by culture, gender, socioeconomic status, or trauma. Development isn't a ladder, and students are capable of great and moral acts (or terrible ones) at any age. Our goal for children is the same as for ourselves—it is to have strategies to constantly reach for our best selves, and to catch ourselves when we stop reaching.

The social–emotional learning approach emphasizes a caring community and consists of classroom and schoolwide practices for deliberately helping children build social–emotional competencies. Programs like the Responsive Classroom Approach and Developmental Designs have made social–emotional learning more accessible. Yet, SEL programs are implemented in only a small fraction of schools nationwide. Often, schools adopt some of the practices, but they are implemented at the surface level and then are not effective. How many times have I heard educators equate teaching SEL and having morning meetings at their school?

SCENARIO First-Grade Classroom, Language Arts Class

"First graders, it is so quiet in here! I can tell by your eyes on your work and your pens moving that you are so focused. Wow! Great job getting right to work. Let's keep it just like this for the next fifteen minutes so that everyone can concentrate and get their best work done. I'm going to be working with the blue table, so if you forget at any point what your job is, the chart on the chart stand will remind you, so remember to look back at it." Ryan, the teacher, sits down with the students at the blue table who need the work modified. As he works with them, he scans the room and notices a student slumped on his arm and who has only written a few words. He excuses himself from the blue table and kneels next to Tadeo and whispers, "Tadeo, what is your job right now?"

"To write my personal story," Tadeo answers.

"Tadeo, show me where you can remind yourself of the steps you need to follow to do the work." Tadeo points to the chart on the chart stand. "That's right. Remember, you have been working really hard on managing your time and your work on your own! I know you can do this without me, so before I go back to the blue table, I'm going to watch you reread the chart so you remember what to do. Then you'll get started on your writing. I'll check in with you in five minutes. You can do this—go!"

Tadeo gives an enthusiastic nod and almost skips to his workplace. He picks up his pen to start working.

The underlying values in this particular SEL classroom are self-awareness and self-management. For a teacher who really knows SEL, that does not mean teaching children to just follow rules. The teacher here is focused on making sure students can be responsible for knowing and doing their own work, and although students are given clear feedback and acknowledgment, they are neither rewarded nor punished. The teaching here is building toward efficacy—I have a plan for my work (and if I forget the plan I know where to get reminded) and know how to get it done. Children in a true SEL approach are participants in the conversation, and they are acquiring skills that can allow then to be joyful and successful without being controlled. They are developing efficacy and becoming people who can make the world a better place.

How to Identify Social–Emotional Learning: Continuum Tool

At SOAR Charter School in Denver, I worked with a group of K–5 teachers who wanted a tool that would guide them in knowing what behavioral indicators students should be demonstrating in regards to the five SEL competencies, by age and grade level. Too often in their practice, they felt unsure of what behaviors they should be looking for, and whether they were expecting too much or too little of students.

Their hope was to use this tool in two ways:

- to evaluate class and individual strengths and weaknesses to craft a plan for supporting students in competency development
- to layer appropriate social and emotional learning targets into daily instruction. In other words, when teaching a reading workshop about partner reading, to intentionally teach something to students about, for example, relationship skills.

We met several times to construct the document. I began with CASEL's definitions of the competencies across the top of the tool. Along the left, I listed the grade levels the school served as well as the range of ages within each grade. When we met the first time we simply came to a shared understanding of what each competency means. At the second meeting, we brainstormed indicators we would *hope* to see in the school setting at a particular grade level. We did so with the understanding that the indicators are

- brief, specific, and observable
- stated as a positive
- cross-checked with other SEL developmental resources for "reliability" (Chip Wood's Yardsticks, Responsive Classroom's What Every Teacher Needs to Know series)
- the result of the child having been taught (through direct teaching, through modeling or some other method, in or out of school)
- to be demonstrated by children who learn and develop at different paces, and as such, we should expect demonstration of the indicators by different children at different points in the school year.

After drafting the tool, there was a trial run. The idea here was that teachers would select one or two students who they believe are developing at an appropriate rate to observe using the grade-level indicators and ask the question, "Is this really what I see?" At the third meeting, we used the observation data to revise the tool. We also decided it was best to revise by competency, rather than grade level, so we could think about the development of the competency over time. For example, let's think about *responsible decision making*. We may see seven-year-olds with a really strong sense of routines that drives their decision making. At eight, they may start to wonder why particular rules and routines exist. Nine-year-olds may argue about how to carry out rules, procedures, and directions. At ten, they are critiquing the fairness of rules, and by eleven, pushing against them as a way to understand them. How empowering it must be for the teacher of the eight-year-old who understands where her students were at seven and where they are heading to at eleven. That kind of understanding can be downright powerful in terms of how in tune we are with student behaviors and how we coach them forward to next stages of understanding and development.

At the end of the process, the team felt that the tool was so powerful that we came up with a list of recommended uses for the school community. For the pilot year, staff would work toward schoolwide understanding of the tool. Teachers would choose between one and six students to assess at multiple points in the year and would track student growth and development across the year. In time, as teachers gained familiarity with the tool, they'd have a list of other potential uses, such as:

- Teachers might select a weekly focus area related to the competencies. For example, if teaching self-management, they might spend a week studying with students how to regulate voices in different settings— libraries, classrooms, playgrounds, concerts, and so on. This might begin with directly teaching about what kind of talk is appropriate in different places—when we should whisper, shout, speak conversationally, or be silent. The teacher could then create a variety of opportunities for practice, with quick transitions to the school playground, then to the library, then to the lunchroom, then to a book talk.
- Teachers and students might select a focus area for self-study. This might mean starting with questions, such as: How are we doing in terms of

social awareness? Are we in tune with how others are thinking or feeling? Do we know how our behavior impacts others? These questions could be the start to a powerful year of lessons, conversations, and student reflections that lead to significant student gains in a competency area of choice.

• The competencies could drive conversations with parents and would be introduced to parents at the first parent–teacher conference. Parents might be asked to share what they see from their children at home, and teachers would share what they are seeing at school. Collaborative plans could be made with parents to support student social–emotional development at home and at school. For example, teacher and parent might agree that using kind language with peers is a need. They might set a goal with the child around this need and give frequent feedback to the child about progress they are making. Teacher and parent would also check in with each other to share strategies and progress.

Although this tool can be used in any school, more importantly, this process can also be replicated in any school. The resulting tool is really the result of the learning that occurred by a group of teachers who want to understand how children develop SEL competencies over time and how to support them.

About the SOAR SEL Continuum (pages 28 through 33)

SOAR's SEL continuum measures student progress against CASEL's five social–emotional learning (SEL) competencies. At each grade level, there is a range of age and developmental indicators. Not all students will exhibit the indicators documented below in the same time frame. If students are on target, generally, they will exhibit all indicators by the end of a grade. However, some students will have indicators above or below their grade level. Note that this continuum is to be used as an assessment and an instructional planning tool. It is a living document that should grow and change over time. Assume that all indicators are a result of teaching inside or outside of school. SEL competencies are not something we are born with. They are learned behaviors.

SOAR SEL CONTINUUM   Kindergarten and Grade 1

SELF-AWARENESS   The ability to accurately recognize one's emotions and thoughts and their influence on behavior. This includes accurately assessing one's strengths and limitations and possessing a well-grounded sense of confidence and optimism.

SELF-MANAGEMENT   The ability to regulate one's emotions, thoughts, and behaviors effectively in different situations. This includes managing stress, controlling impulses, motivating oneself, and setting and working toward achieving personal and academic goals.

KINDERGARTEN
(4–6 years old)

Self-Awareness:
- ☐ Comfortable with close contact of peers and adults
- ☐ Prefers the familiar—repetition of choice or activity or book reading
- ☐ Enjoys structured games
- ☐ Uses sentence stems effectively to briefly express emotions ("I don't like it when . . . because it makes me feel . . .")
- ☐ Recognizes accomplishments and understands the value behind them
- ☐ Proud of following rules

Self-Management:
- ☐ Follows two- or three-step directions with ease
- ☐ Can use a visual tool (e.g., schedule) to help them cope with stress
- ☐ Cries easily when upset but can make quick transition to being able to participate productively

GRADE 1
(5–7 years old)

Self-Awareness:
- ☐ Can identify and articulate simple behavioral and academic challenges
- ☐ Tries to use known problem-solving strategies
- ☐ Motivated by getting things right
- ☐ Likes to be first, as accomplishments are increasingly important
- ☐ Can identify simple needs in a conflict situation
- ☐ Enjoys increased responsibility for self and others
- ☐ Loves very active play

Self-Management:
- ☐ Follows multistep directions without confusion
- ☐ Makes quick transitions from being upset to a new activity
- ☐ Responds well to nonverbal redirection
- ☐ Unaware of body/voice control

SOCIAL AWARENESS   The ability to take the perspective of and empathize with others from diverse backgrounds and cultures, to understand social and ethical norms for behavior, and to recognize family, school, and community resources and supports.

RELATIONSHIP SKILLS   The ability to establish and maintain healthy and rewarding relationships with diverse individuals and groups. This includes communicating clearly, listening actively, cooperating, resisting inappropriate social pressure, negotiating conflict constructively, and seeking and offering help when needed.

RESPONSIBLE DECISION MAKING The ability to make constructive and respectful choices about personal behavior and social interactions based on consideration of ethical standards, safety concerns, social norms, the realistic evaluation of consequences of various actions, and the well-being of self and others.

☐ Likes to please adults

☐ Reads body language to understand the emotions of others

☐ Says "please" and "thank you"

☐ Comfortable sharing and taking turns during lessons

☐ Notices and names physical differences among peers

☐ Notices and easily adjusts to the differences in home vs. school culture

☐ Easily transitions to new relationships with adults and children

☐ Social talk is excited and focused on own shares

☐ Primary relationships are with family and teacher, not as much with other students

☐ Follows stated rules

☐ Use sentence stems to hold self and other students accountable to rules

☐ Responsibly picks between behavioral choices

☐ Uses adult modeling for decision making about rules and boundaries

☐ Relies on understood routines to make decisions

☐ Tries to comfort others who are upset with physical or verbal outreach (e.g., puts arm around shoulder, or asks, "Are you okay?")

☐ Talk is excited and focused on input

☐ Makes good use of sentence stems in social and academic situations (e.g., start of an apology)

☐ Beginning to recognize when their actions have emotional impact on others

☐ Sympathetic with others

☐ Will notice and vocalize what is or is not fair

☐ Enjoys gender-based friendships

☐ Notices misbehavior of others

☐ Easily transitions to new relationships with adults and children

☐ Wants to help other students and the teacher

☐ Cares deeply about friends—worried about students who are absent, may have a best friend

☐ Makes responsible decisions about work partners or groups

☐ Uses peer behavior for decision making about rules and boundaries

☐ Trying to determine their relationship with authority; where they have independence/choice, and where they need to follow stated rules

☐ Tries to establish own way of doing things, makes own rules

☐ Uses sentence stems to hold self and other students accountable to rules

SOAR SEL Continuum   Grades 2 and 3

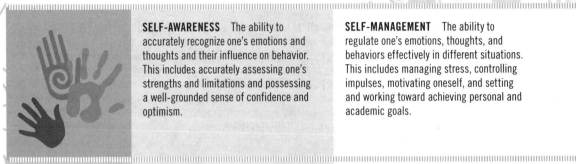

SELF-AWARENESS The ability to accurately recognize one's emotions and thoughts and their influence on behavior. This includes accurately assessing one's strengths and limitations and possessing a well-grounded sense of confidence and optimism.

SELF-MANAGEMENT The ability to regulate one's emotions, thoughts, and behaviors effectively in different situations. This includes managing stress, controlling impulses, motivating oneself, and setting and working toward achieving personal and academic goals.

Grade 2
(6–8 years old)

Self-Awareness
- ☐ Can identify positive or negative emotions related to an event that is in progress (e.g., "I get nervous in math because I am bad at it and never know the answer")
- ☐ Knows chores/tasks they are responsible for and completes them
- ☐ Enjoys board games, secrets/codes, inventing
- ☐ Wants work to be perfect
- ☐ Enjoys alone time, confined or private work spaces, and own set of materials
- ☐ Greater gross motor control, resulting in very physical play

Self-Management
- ☐ Can quickly transition from being upset to calming down (e.g., high frustration when a table mate doesn't share scissors, but once scissors are attained, quickly moves into the activity)
- ☐ Negotiates rules in play ("in basketball today tackling is allowed, but then you can never call a foul")
- ☐ Is beginning to be able to set own consequences but may not be logical
- ☐ Cares about contributing to classroom community through jobs, being a good friend, academic contributions
- ☐ Developing awareness of body/voice control

Grade 3
(7–9 years old)

Self-Awareness
- ☐ Willing to take academic risks
- ☐ Can name and advocate for classroom conditions they need to be successful (e.g., private work space, support, etc.)
- ☐ Takes feedback to heart
- ☐ Thrives on teacher encouragement, lightness, and humor
- ☐ Enjoys physical play, structured games, team sports
- ☐ Aware of regulating behavior in a variety of settings
- ☐ Enjoys space/time away from teachers/ authority

Self-Management
- ☐ Adjusts easily to changes in groupings, teams, etc.
- ☐ Able to set and accept logical consequences for behavior
- ☐ Applies teacher feedback
- ☐ Can readily apply stress reduction techniques to manage upset feelings
- ☐ Awareness of body/voice control in regards to social norms

SOCIAL AWARENESS   The ability to take the perspective of and empathize with others from diverse backgrounds and cultures, to understand social and ethical norms for behavior, and to recognize family, school, and community resources and supports.

RELATIONSHIP SKILLS   The ability to establish and maintain healthy and rewarding relationships with diverse individuals and groups. This includes communicating clearly, listening actively, cooperating, resisting inappropriate social pressure, negotiating conflict constructively, and seeking and offering help when needed.

RESPONSIBLE DECISION MAKING
The ability to make constructive and respectful choices about personal behavior and social interactions based on consideration of ethical standards, safety concerns, social norms, the realistic evaluation of consequences of various actions, and the well-being of self and others.

- ☐ Increasingly aware of how friends are feeling
- ☐ Tries to comfort friends who are upset
- ☐ Exhibits good manners—says "please," "thank you"
- ☐ Sometimes independently takes turns in social situations
- ☐ Developing understanding of differences between self and peers—race, culture, religion, preferences
- ☐ Empathetic, especially with close friends
- ☐ Generally sympathetic with upset peers

- ☐ Individual, rather than group, friendships are increasingly important
- ☐ Recognizes qualities that make a good friend
- ☐ Affectionate with friends
- ☐ May change friends frequently
- ☐ Focused on getting their "fair share"
- ☐ Will allow teachers to facilitate friendships or partnerships
- ☐ May rely on adults for problem solving

- ☐ Can make decisions about who to work with and where to work in a responsible way
- ☐ Strong sense of routines
- ☐ Increasing interest in why rules exist
- ☐ Is aware of rule-breaking behavior
- ☐ Willing to make decisions to try new experiences
- ☐ Needs frequent check-ins with the teacher

- ☐ Increasingly social
- ☐ Exhibits good manners—says "please," "thank you," "I'm sorry"
- ☐ Takes turns when talking in a social situation and with the teacher
- ☐ Conscious of how their peers perceive them
- ☐ Uses language intentionally to impact others
- ☐ Empathetic with situations they are familiar with or can immediately relate to

- ☐ Invites others to play
- ☐ Actively disagrees without arguing
- ☐ Moves on easily from disagreements
- ☐ Forms friendships out of a specific shared interest/experience
- ☐ Enjoys competing with others in play
- ☐ Begins to solve own conflicts
- ☐ Asks for academic and social help when needed
- ☐ Peer relationships more important than relationships with adults

- ☐ Deliberates over rules/procedures of activities
- ☐ Desire to "make deals"
- ☐ Increasing awareness of right and wrong
- ☐ Beginning to understand fair is not always equal
- ☐ Articulates reasoning for decision making

SOAR SEL CONTINUUM   Grades 4 and 5

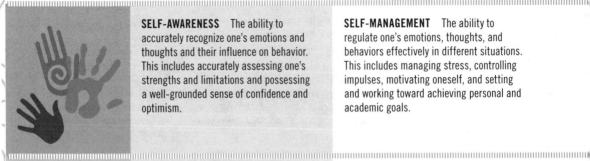

	SELF-AWARENESS The ability to accurately recognize one's emotions and thoughts and their influence on behavior. This includes accurately assessing one's strengths and limitations and possessing a well-grounded sense of confidence and optimism.	**SELF-MANAGEMENT** The ability to regulate one's emotions, thoughts, and behaviors effectively in different situations. This includes managing stress, controlling impulses, motivating oneself, and setting and working toward achieving personal and academic goals.
GRADE 4 (8–10 years old)	☐ Is clear about personal likes and dislikes ☐ Can identify events that *will* trigger negative or positive emotions (e.g., "I know that anytime I get caught not doing the right thing, I get very emotional. I have outbursts and do not take responsibility for my actions when I know a loss of privilege is coming") ☐ Understands personal responsibility for and sense of accomplishment in completing chores/tasks ☐ Detail oriented, often motivated by creating an "end project" ☐ Choice (academic, social, and play) is increasingly important ☐ Enjoys structured activities ☐ Understands behaviors expected in a variety of settings and social situations ☐ Enjoys space/time with peers away from teachers/authority	☐ Can use personal strategies to calm down when upset (deep breathing, walking away from a situation) ☐ Regulates emotions in response to broken rules in play, or winning or losing (can congratulate the opponent's efforts whether winning or losing, can rein in gloating) ☐ Asks for help when it is truly needed ☐ Can exhibit patience while waiting ☐ Accepts feedback productively
GRADE 5 (9–11 years old)	☐ Shares personal likes and dislikes with others ☐ Uses strategies to trigger positive rather than negative emotions (e.g., follows a system for organizing materials rather than getting upset that materials will get lost) ☐ Is aware of needs for privacy/personal space ☐ Cares about personal accomplishment (e.g., personal performance in academics, sports, arts) ☐ Enjoys competition, team sports, brain teasers, logic games, board games	☐ Can make plan for implementing feedback ☐ Competes (e.g., playground) without getting upset ☐ Can use personal strategies to calm down when upset (deep breathing, walking away from a situation) ☐ Can readily regulate outward display of emotions ☐ Asks for help when it is truly needed ☐ Exhibits patience while waiting

SOCIAL AWARENESS The ability to take the perspective of and empathize with others from diverse backgrounds and cultures, to understand social and ethical norms for behavior, and to recognize family, school, and community resources and supports.

RELATIONSHIP SKILLS The ability to establish and maintain healthy and rewarding relationships with diverse individuals and groups. This includes communicating clearly, listening actively, cooperating, resisting inappropriate social pressure, negotiating conflict constructively, and seeking and offering help when needed.

RESPONSIBLE DECISION MAKING The ability to make constructive and respectful choices about personal behavior and social interactions based on consideration of ethical standards, safety concerns, social norms, the realistic evaluation of consequences of various actions, and the well-being of self and others.

- ☐ Exhibits good manners—says "please," "thank you," "excuse me," "I'm sorry" appropriately
- ☐ Understands how own behavior may impact others (e.g., being fidgety, etc.)
- ☐ Is aware of needs for privacy/space
- ☐ Increasing awareness of and openness to differences: cultural, religious, gender, sexual preference
- ☐ Understands one's words and actions have social power
- ☐ Can more readily empathize with others
- ☐ Is beginning to question purpose of rules

- ☐ Appreciates and can move on when reparations are made
- ☐ Compromises on how to spend time together
- ☐ Takes longer to recover from personal loss (e.g., divorce, teacher leaving, death, etc.)
- ☐ Increasing awareness of and desire to interact with other genders
- ☐ Noticing/development of popularity
- ☐ Beginning to evaluate the quality of their friendships

- ☐ Heightened awareness of right and wrong
- ☐ Generally truthful
- ☐ Understands the connection between positive behavior and privileges
- ☐ Able to consider the long-term impact of their decisions
- ☐ Can make good decisions about who to productively work and play with
- ☐ Influenced by how others will perceive them

- ☐ Feels badly for peers who have negative interactions with teachers or peers
- ☐ Is angered by historical injustice
- ☐ Has heightened awareness of own biases and is open minded about discussing them
- ☐ Stands up for others in the face of bullying
- ☐ Can easily recognize that they have caused a problem and take action to fix it
- ☐ Interested in learning more about other cultures, engages in debates about differences
- ☐ Interested in exploring the purpose and logic of rules and authority

- ☐ Introduces self in new situations
- ☐ Independently creates distance between self and peers when peers are misbehaving
- ☐ Accepts as a matter of fact that personal likes and dislikes of others may be different from own
- ☐ Takes longer to recover from personal loss
- ☐ Needs more private social time with peers
- ☐ More likely to stop being friends with people who don't treat them well

- ☐ Invites others to planned conversations to solve problems (e.g., asks to meet with the teacher to discuss an interpersonal issue, subject concern, etc.)
- ☐ Evolving sense of right and wrong, so needs think time for making decisions
- ☐ Is thoughtful about how decisions will affect self and others (e.g., "I know friends will be disappointed if I go to basketball practice over sleepover")
- ☐ Pushes back on authority as a way to establish/define identity and personal boundaries

Rewards and Consequences Don't Work

Before we get into the nitty-gritty of *what to do*, let's examine what research tells us about *what not to do* and *why not*. A common practice in classrooms is to use some type of reward or token system to manage behavior. In other words, it becomes an "If you do this, I'll give you (or take away) that" system. Typically, these systems look effective because they have the short-term result of controlling students' behavior (Elias and Schwab 2006). Yet, they miss the mark because they do not support children's internal motivation to be an independent learner (Reeve 2006). The student may focus on the expected reward rather than improving their social–emotional or academic abilities (Reeve 2006).

One extreme example of a rewards and consequences (namely consequences) approach is the zero tolerance policy. According to the American Psychological Association (APA) Zero Tolerance Task Force (2008), zero tolerance "became widely adopted in schools in the early 1990s as a philosophy or policy that mandates the application of predetermined consequences, most often severe and punitive in nature, that are intended to be applied regardless of the gravity of behavior, mitigating circumstances, or situational context" (1). The APA task force report indicates that schools that institute zero tolerance policies have lower school climate ratings and lower academic achievement.

Demands, whether delivered by a reward or punishment, are about imposing one's will on another. When we do that, we actually freeze the child in their default mode of compliance or oppositional behavior—we don't help them grow. Instead, our mental model of classroom management needs to be a conversation, and, to be a successful conversation, we need to see the value of more than one approach in a given context and more than one voice in the conversation.

SCENARIO   Rewards and Consequences Conversation: Second-Grade, Language Arts Class

"Nice job getting to your tables, second graders, and getting right to work. Every table just earned two table points." Ms. Allen says, waving her two hands in the air in a silent cheer. The children respond back with silent cheers of their own. The children work quietly as Ms. Allen circulates, looking over their shoulders. At a table behind her, she hears two students talking. She turns toward them. "Jacinda and Alex, that is the second time this morning. Go move your cards from green to yellow." Jacinda looks contrite, but Alex puts her head down on the table and begins to cry.

Rewards and consequences is an age-old approach. So old that China's early interpreters of Taoism, Zhuangzi, who lived from 389–286C, said, "Rewards and punishment is the lowest form of education." Rewards and consequences are two sides of the same coin." On one side, think treasure chests, pizza parties, or stickers; on the other think stoplights, trips to the office, and loss of recess.

Some educators live by the rewards and consequences approach for its immediacy, although others are opposed to the extrinsic nature of the methodology. This model values compliance through carrots and sticks. What kind of person might a child who learns in a rewards and consequences model become? Perhaps an adult who is compliant when the reward is the right one—one who says, what will I get for doing this? And who conversely makes decisions to avoid getting in trouble. Again, this just doesn't fit the mental model of classroom management as a conversation. It is a manipulative approach focused on controlling children through carrots and sticks.

SCENARIO   Conversation in a Fifth-Grade, Language Arts Class: "No Excuses"—A "Consequence-Heavy" Approach

Students, seated in rows, are neatly dressed in khaki trousers, burgundy polo shirts, and black shoes. Mr. Orchard walks to the front of the room and faces the class. "Good morning, scholars." The class stands and in unison and responds, "Good morning, Mr. Orchard," to which Mr. Orchard responds, "You may sit." And then, "Take out your writing skills book and turn to page 5. You have ten minutes to practice sentence diagramming. The timer is set. Begin."

Mr. Orchard walks up and down the rows as students work. He notices a student staring off at something other than his workbook, with no marks on his page. "Xavion," he says for the class to hear, "One demerit for not getting started. If you get one more, you will have five for the week, and that will mean you will do this work on Saturday. Now get to work."

No excuses is a term that means that educators do not accept that the countless problems that have plagued public education can be accepted as excuses for why children do not succeed. It focuses on uniform adherence to rules and consistent consequences. The name itself—*no excuses*—suggests that children or families might be "trying to get out of" something. Was Xavion trying to get out of something, might not he have understood the work, or might it have been too easy for him? Could there have been some trauma or worry that kept him from being focused? But no excuses means exactly that—do exactly what you are told to do when you are told to do it, without question or argument. If you don't do it well enough, fast enough, the way you were told to, there will be a consequence—demerits, detention, or some other punishment.

Here, expectations and consequences are doled out uniformly, no matter who you are or what you bring to the table. The underlying message is comply and assimilate. And achieve—the teaching is focused on high standardized test scores and college attendance, because without those, students cannot be successful. If you can't put in the effort, if you need something different than the other students, if you are going to make excuses—this approach will not serve you.

The no excuses approach has gained recent popularity in the media. The approach is believed to have started with The Knowledge Is Power Program (KIPP) and adopted by other "high-performing" charter schools. Movies like *Waiting for Superman* and authors like Paul Tough have popularized the "no excuses" approach and the development of "grit" as a student characteristic.

This is a controversial approach, though, tied to the current political education agenda. P. L. Thomas of the National Center for Education Policy (2013) writes:

> In the race to the top that public education has become, affluent children . . . have the slack necessary to fail, to quit, and to try again. . . . Children in poverty do not have such slack . . . their cognitive and emotional resources are drained, preoccupied. The ugly little secret behind calls for "no excuses" and "grit" is that achievement is the result of slack, not grit.

What kind of person might a child who learns in a no excuses model become? A compliant adult who doesn't believe in rocking the boat, who wants to fit in, who is fearful of consequences, who respects "authority," who strives for accomplishments? That isn't my vision for children. That's an adult-only conversation that excludes the interests of the child. It's a one-way street where the adult controls the outcomes for the child.

Any classroom management system can have something to offer when it is used flexibly. But no matter the approach, we want students to develop, through direct and supportive instruction, the social–emotional competencies that are critical for their long-term success: self-awareness, self-management, social awareness, positive relationship skills, and responsible decision making. As a result of learning these skills, children can develop into complete people who can lead effectual lives—lives in which they not only advocate for themselves but affect change for others. In an ideal school, the competencies create the underpinnings of the school's classroom management approach.

As a result of developing these skills, dispositions, and competencies, children can mature into complete people who can lead effectual lives. But that isn't easy work. First and foremost, it requires an unwavering belief that SEL competencies are learned. It requires assessment practices that allow teachers to determine class needs as well as individual student needs. It also requires a plan for teaching. And as with all good teaching, there needs to be a feedback loop to students and follow-up teaching.

3

How Do I Set Boundaries and Teach Expectations?

Gentle in what you do, firm in how you do it.

—BUCK BRANNAMAN (translation from Latin, *Solvitur en modo, firmitur en rey*)

If you have children of your own, you will know that every parenting magazine, book, or article speaks to the need for parents to establish clear and predictable boundaries—around behavior, eating, chores, bedtime—you name it. Again and again, whether it is from Doctor Sears, Doctor Spock, or a long list of other doctors and psychologists, boundaries help children feel safe. Boundaries help children learn how to understand their environment and regulate their behavior within it. Without boundaries, children can't be successful. Again and again, parenting experts say, don't get caught up in wanting your child to like you—get caught up in what is best for your child. For teachers, this same advice should hold true.

But the word *boundaries* itself is difficult for some adults, who interpret it as a line that cannot be crossed, excessively limiting and rigid. Although I appreciate any pushback on rigidity, I think that concern is a misinterpretation of who boundaries serve. Boundaries might feel rigid to the adult, but for the child they are expectations, not limits. Healthy adults set boundaries all the time—with our parents, with our pets, with our partners, friends, and children. Setting boundaries means being clear with yourself about behaviors that are reasonable, safe, and tolerable. Without them, we would fail at most endeavors.

And yet it's true that not just children struggle with boundaries. Often adults do. In fact, what I hope you gain from this chapter is an understanding of how much you or a colleague's difficulty with classroom behavior can be avoided when you set boundaries. Let's first identify some of the reasons teachers give for not doing this work (Figure 3–1). As you can see, behind each of these reasons is a fear. That tells us that these teachers simply need some support in understanding how to envision and establish safe and respectful boundaries.

I've had even the most experienced teachers tell me that setting boundaries is the most exhausting part of teaching, because the boundaries will always be tested. While I understand this frustration, I have another way of thinking about it that has made setting boundaries seem much less frustrating. Allan Hamilton, who is a brain surgeon and horseman, uses horses to teach doctors about better ways of interacting with their patients as well as teaching business leaders and teachers about more effective communication and leadership. He's explains the left-brained human tendency to believe you *deserve* something, to the right-brained tendency to need to *earn* something, using *Otancan*, the Lakota word for leader. He teaches people that in the world of horses, if you are the horse's Otancan, the horse has two obligations. The first is to follow you. The second is to challenge you. This isn't because the horse is being "bad." The horse needs to know there is a herd leader for survival—and if you aren't the leader, the horse will be. When you don't know this, you might become really upset that the horse is challenging you and begin to question yourself and the horse. You might even get angry and punitive. But if instead you know a challenge will come, you are prepared to gently and firmly remind him that yes, you are indeed still the leader and will keep him safe. What an empowering change in mind-set!

Teachers say	Which really means
It's mean.	I want the kids to like me and they won't if I am too bossy.
It's not my personality.	I haven't done this before or I am out of my comfort zone.
They can't.	I am intimidated and afraid of failure.

Figure 3–1. What's Behind "I'm Not Comfortable with Setting Boundaries"

Although humans and horses are different, two essential facts remain the same. The first is that no one deserves eternal leadership with unquestioning followers—leadership must be earned. The second is that human beings challenge their leaders—be it their parents, teachers, principals, or president. When teachers can say, "I know a challenge is coming every day, no big deal. I'm ready for it" and will remain gentle but firm to keep their students safe and productive, then they are true leaders who have mastered the art of setting boundaries. My hope is this chapter will give you some useful and practical advice for doing just that to make your classrooms more productive learning spaces for children. Let's delve into what the research can tell us about objective reasons children need us to do this.

Any Expected Behavior Must Be Taught

Just as we teach academic expectations, we must teach behavioral expectations. There are several ways to do this. First, effective teachers are proactive! That is, they prevent problem behavior before it occurs. Having clear and predictable routines and rules is a way to increase your students' positive behaviors (Epstein et al. 2008; Kern and Clemens 2007). Students' misbehavior may be due to unclear classroom expectations (Bullara 1993; Mayer 1995). Routines and rules should be explicitly taught *and* practiced. When this is done, children are more on task and exhibit less problem behavior (Gettinger and Kohler 2006; Kern and Clemens 2007). Additionally, before a task is begun (e.g., lining up to go to lunch, transitioning from whole group to small group), teachers should remind students about the expectations (Emmer, Evertson, and Anderson 1980; Mayer 1995; Stormont, Smith, and Lewis 2007).

Second, you should provide positive reinforcement when students meet your expectations. Positive reinforcement provides your students feedback about their behavior, which builds their feelings of competence (Reeve 2006). When students feel more competent about their abilities, they are more likely to *continue* to exhibit positive behavior (Kern and Clemens 2007; Montague and Renaldi 2001). Thus, we as teachers are developing a self-fulfilling prophecy in the desired direction! Praise should always be sincerely delivered (Hester, Hendrickson, and Gable, 2009). It is important to be systematic about the frequency with which you deliver positive reinforcement. Teachers *should* provide praise four times as often as they provide corrective feedback (Kern and Clemens 2007). Yet, Sutherland

and Wehby (2001) found that teachers actually do the reverse; they reprimand three times as often as they praised. Fortunately, when teachers recorded their own use of reprimands and reinforcement behaviors, they increased their praise statements and decreased their reprimands (Sutherland and Wehby 2001).

Third, teachers need a systematic plan to address misbehavior once it occurs. Even with explicit teaching of rules/procedures and provision of positive reinforcement, students are still going to misbehave. When this occurs, teachers should immediately redirect students using positive and direct language (Matheson and Shriver 2005; Walker and Sylwester 1998). It is best practice for teachers to tell students what to do (i.e., "Walk" or "Use kind words with your friend") versus what not to do (e.g., "Do not run" or "Don't tease"). A common mistake that teachers make is forming their redirection as a question, like "Amya, can you return to your seat?" This is known as an indirect command. Some students, particularly low-income and minority students, may not understand that an indirect command *is* a redirection, rather than a legitimate question (Morine-Dershimer 2006).

When students do not follow the rules, there need to be clear and consistent consequences. As previously mentioned, a rewards and consequences approach is not effective; it serves to control students' behavior. In these classrooms, consequences are typically uniform across children and situations. In other words, any child who misbehaves for any reason (except egregious behavior like threats or violence) is issued the same consequences: a verbal warning, strike one (name on board), strike two (note or phone call home), and so on. However, when issued properly, consequences provide students with the opportunities to learn and practice more appropriate ways of behaving (Bohn, Roehrig, and Pressley 2004; Gettinger and Kohler 2006; Landrum and Kauffman 2006). Consequences should be reasonable and relate to the misbehavior (Elias and Schwab 2006; Watson and Ecken 2003). Consequences are best delivered calmly and privately (Elias and Schwab 2006; Landrum and Kauffman 2006). If reprimanded publically, students may feel embarrassed or angry, which is harmful to the close teacher–student relationship you are trying to develop (Landrum and Kauffman 2006; Woolfolk-Hoy and Weinstein 2006).

When communicating with students, it is best to get physically close to and make eye contact with students (Emmer, Evertson, and Anderson 1980; Rhode, Jenson, and Morgan 2009; Shores, Gunter, and Jack 1993). Feedback to students about their behavior should be specific and immediate (Bohn, Roehrig, and Pressley 2004; Stormont, Smith, and Lewis 2007). In addition, teachers should communicate to students in a calm and respectful tone of voice (Matheson and Shriver 2005; Rhode, Jenson, and Morgan 2009).

How to Teach Expected Behaviors Through Classroom Rules and Procedures

Teachers of well-managed classrooms have a vision for what each part of the day should look like, and they communicate expectations and create procedures to make their vision a reality. For example, they think through the steps of how a perfect pack-up at the end of the day would go. Where would students be when it is time to pack up? What might they be finishing? How do they get to their bags and coats? When and how do they get the materials that go into their backpack? Do they go one at a time or in groups? How will you send them so that the flow of movement is safe and controlled? What do they do when they are finished packing up?

The teaching of classroom procedures should be approached as systematically and methodically as teaching academic content. When procedures are thoroughly taught, children are more on task and exhibit less misbehavior.

Nothing that happens in the classroom is too small or too insignificant for a carefully planned procedure. Think through everything (everything!) that a student must do over the course of a school day. If you can name it, it deserves a thoughtful procedure that you can teach to the student. Students should never have to guess how you want them to do something. I'll name a few times of day I have seen teachers forget to make a procedure for and then we can think through one or two of them:

- the time between when students enter into the classroom and instruction begins
- snack time
- going to the bathroom
- walking in the halls
- independent work time
- coming back into the classroom after recess.

So let's think about coming back from recess. I've had lots of teachers say to me that kids are so wound up after recess that getting them to a place where they are ready for instruction again may or may not happen. The first thing is, how many procedures is this really? I'd say three—lining up on the playground, walking back to the classroom, and entering the classroom. For the greatest success, I would teach about each procedure separately, and then connect them. For sure, a problem lining up will contribute to a problem walking back to the classroom, which will contribute to a problem entering the classroom. For now, let's assume the problem starts right when students have the classroom in sight. They ask the teacher for water, ask to use the bathroom, complain that they are sweaty, ask what the class is going to do now, complain that so-and-so did such-and-so on the playground. I've seen that happen. See Figure 3–2 for questions that can help when creating procedures.

Sometimes it is hard to be as precise as you really need to be to get a crisp, efficient procedure. When I worked through this process with a teacher, here is how it went.

Imagine the Procedure: What Should It Look Like, Sound Like?

I want students to stop right outside the classroom door. I want them to stay in their lines, get very quiet, and turn their bodies toward me to look at me while they wait for my directions. *What will your directions be,* I ask, *and I suggest that at least for a few weeks, the directions are very simple, and very consistent.* When I say "Go," they will enter the room, get out their math notebooks and a pen out of their

---

Here are the questions you need to work through for fixing any procedure:

» What do you want it to look like? Sound like? Be precise from start to finish, step by step, as if you are writing a "how-to": first, then, next. . . .
» Are there any changes you will need to make to the environment for this to occur?
» When are you going to introduce this to students?
» How will you introduce it?
» When will students practice?
» How will students know if they are doing a good job?

Figure 3–2. Questions to Help Create Procedures

cubbies, go directly to their seats, and work on the problem that will be written on the dry-erase board. *Will they all enter the room at the same time, and are they allowed to talk?* I'll let about five or six students in at a time, and no, no talking. *For how long?* They will have two to three minutes. And then what? Then I'll ring the chime, and they will come to their carpet spots. *What happens to their materials?* They can bring those to the carpet. I'll always start by reviewing the problem with them. *Is anyone allowed to get water or go to the bathroom during this time?* No.

Do I need to change the environment for this to occur?

Yes, I'll need to make sure we clean out the cubbies so math notebooks are easy to get to. I also need to make sure water bottles stay at tables so kids can drink water as they need.

When and how am I going to introduce this to students?

I think I'll do it as part of the morning updates. After we have our morning meeting, I'll tell them about the change in procedure. That way, there are several hours between them hearing about it and recess. If the students react to the change, I have time to discuss it before they are rushing out the door.

When will students practice?

We'll practice once right at morning updates, and then again after reading workshop. I'll model the procedure once and have students share their observations of what I did. Then I'll have a small group try it, then everyone.

After reading workshop, I'll remind them again of how the procedure is supposed to go, and we'll practice again. Hopefully, two practices before the real thing will be enough. But if the practices don't go well, I'll have them do it over once each time. I'll make it brief so it doesn't feel like a chore.

How will students know if they are doing a good job?

I'll give lots of positive feedback on whatever they do correctly. *Anything else you can do so they can self-reflect?* Maybe I can make a checklist with the criteria for a good transition, and we can talk about how we did together. Then we can use that all week.

It takes that level of detail to plan out how to fix a procedure that isn't going well, or if there are problematic procedures that are impacting each other (again, recess lineup impacting walking back to the classroom impacting entering the classroom). When teachers are struggling with procedures, I often find that the problem begins with the way students enter the classroom.

Co-create Rules with Your Students

Just because you co-create rules with your students doesn't mean they will follow them. However, the co-creation gives you a shared context for revisiting rules when you see that children have more learning to do—and they will!—around the rules. Just as it is important that students have some say in their academic learning, because it results in greater investment, they should have a say in the rules they will be expected to live by.

You can let students brainstorm the rules they think are important to keep your classroom community positive and safe. They may come up with hundreds, mostly stated as what you shouldn't do, and that is okay. They might say:

- Don't talk while the teacher is talking.
- Don't run.
- Don't hit.
- Don't kick.
- Don't leave people out on the playground.
- Don't call names.
- Don't play during work time.
- If you drop a pencil, pick it up.
- Do what the teacher says.
- Don't grab materials.

If they each write their top three to five rules down on index cards, you can help them categorize. *Which ones are the same rule? Which ones are similar—rules about talking, how you use your body, rules about how we treat property?* Once you have categories, students can help you write overarching rules that are:

- stated in the positive
- few in number

- posted in a central area
- referred to consistently.

Here is an example:

- Take good care of yourself and your learning.
- Take care of each other's feelings and safety.
- Take care of our classroom and school environment.
- Try everything more than once!

Once rules are posted, you should revisit them to define them more deeply. *Has anyone thought of new ways we can take care of each other's feelings and safety?* If rules aren't referred to often, they are meaningless. For example, "Amanda, I see you've given up on this math problem. Remember our rule to try everything more than once. Let's think of a strategy for multiplying that we have tried before and see if it might work here. . . ."

Always remember that rules aren't meant to micromanage student behavior. They are meant to act as commonly understood guidelines for establishing a joyful and safe classroom where taking risks, making plentiful mistakes, and learning new skills in order to find a better way are part of the daily practice.

Follow Through: Remind, Reinforce, and Redirect

I grew up in a household where one of my father's mantras was "Say what you mean and mean what you say," and that he did. Maybe because of that, the importance of intentional follow-up seems obvious to me. But I have seen that it is not so obvious to everyone.

As an example, one of the schools I worked in had an admirable student snack policy—only fresh fruit and vegetables. And yet in classrooms I worked in, teachers permitted students to eat string cheese, crackers, and potato chips. Curious, I asked the teacher about it, who said she's been doing it for years. When I asked a school administrator how she ensures the policy is followed, her response was, "I follow up when I see it."

This is exactly like what I see happening in classrooms. The teacher who requires students to write their full names and date at the top of every page, but few students do it and the teacher doesn't check; the teacher who assigns seats but doesn't make sure students sit in them until there is a problem; the teacher who creates classroom rules but rarely refers back to them.

It isn't enough to verbalize a policy, procedure, or routine. It isn't enough to state reminders. It isn't enough to "catch it" when you can. Follow through, like everything else, needs to be routinized, intentional, and on your schedule. Students, like adults, make fast decisions about the kind of person you are—one who follows through or one who doesn't. Be the one who says what you mean and means what you say. If you know you won't follow through on something, offer it as a choice, not a directive.

We follow through by intervening at key moments with specific, focused language. The intention of our language should affect the way it sounds. In other words, when we are correcting behavior, it should sound dramatically different than when we compliment children. Words carry greater meaning through volume, intonation, and pacing. Figure 3–3 shows examples of what the teacher might say when establishing this room-entry procedure so that students know how they are doing. Remember that redirecting language is stated in the positive and tells children what to do, not what not to do. And it isn't a question.

Second graders Benny and Sam are sitting at the same table during reading workshop. They have chosen to sit together to do buddy reading. There are a number of choices students have been taught about how to share a big book during buddy reading. For example:

- I read a page aloud, you read a page aloud.
- I read aloud a book this time, you read aloud the book next time.
- We point and read each page together.

Sam and Benny begin arguing about how to read the big book they have chosen— each wants to read the entire book aloud.

A teacher who uses authority to control would make the decision for the students and be done with it. For example, "Sam reads aloud today. Benny reads aloud tomorrow," or worse, "You both are having a problem so no buddy reading for you today—read by yourselves." But a teacher who uses authority to influence might say, "Benny and Sam, you have three choices, which you know well and are outlined on the chart hanging in front of the room. I'm going to give you sixty seconds to review your choices and come to an agreement. If you can't agree, I

Reminding language, to bring students' minds and memory to the task at hand:

» "You are expected to get your notebooks out right now and start math the way we practiced. Show me."

» "I'm turning the timer on. You have thirty seconds to get in your seats, make sure your chairs are carefully tucked under your tables, and begin independent reading. This transition needs to happen quietly. You may begin entering the classroom."

» "Who can name some things we should keep in mind so we all get started quickly and quietly?"

Reinforcing language, to let students know that yes, they've got it!

» "You are showing me that you know how to get started right away—great work getting to your seats, opening your notebooks, and getting right to solving that problem."

» "That was perfect! Everyone was working within twenty seconds, and it was quiet the entire time."

» "We were able to get so much work done today because of the way you entered the classroom. What helped you to be so successful?"

Redirecting language, so students have the opportunity to fix it if it isn't right.

» "Rewind. Come back to the line, and we are going to enter the classroom the way we agreed to."

» "I told you this work is to be done independently, but I see students working with a partner. I expect you to fix that. I'll watch while you do it."

Figure 3–3. Kinds of Teacher Language to Communicate Expectations

will make the decision for you." The teacher set clear boundaries but also offered students a choice and the opportunity to resolve their disagreement on their own. That is reasonable and respectful.

Let's look at a classroom example of a teacher skillfully using her authority to influence student self-management. In this situation, the teacher's use of authority is about both establishing boundaries and teaching self-management.

Alyssa has just taught a reading lesson, and students have been sent off to their own seats for independent reading. Students have been asked to note their thinking in reading notebooks, so they have multiple materials to manage—pens, notebooks, and the books they are each reading. Students know the system for getting and using materials—it has been taught and practiced. Alyssa scans the room to make sure all of the students are on task before she settles in to work with a small group of students. She knows her class well, and takes a moment to see if any of the three to four students who often need individual check-ins before getting on task will need them today.

Xavier has historically struggled with reading. As many children who struggle with academic frustrations do, he acted out in classrooms both out of frustration and as a cover for his own struggles—even to the point of acting physically and verbally aggressive toward other students. Most of his school experience has been characterized by a "me-versus-them" experience with staff. His teacher from last year wanted his Individual Education Plan (IEP) to be changed to reflect that he was emotionally disturbed and for him to be placed in a self-contained classroom, which his parents vehemently opposed. This year, his teacher has made planned efforts to build a positive relationship with him and meet his needs instructionally so Xavier feels like he has an ally. He knows this about her, and his affection for her is growing, but history has made him wary. One step she has taken was to help him select books that on the outside look "mature" (he was embarrassed to read "baby books") and have high interest and appropriate readability. Xavier and Alyssa have agreed to a goal of him getting started with his work right away. She watches this carefully to be sure that altercations between Xavier and other students don't occur. This is not a goal he has yet begun meeting independently, but on this day, he sees Alyssa watching and signaling him with her eyes and gestures to get to it, so he takes his seat, opens his book and gets to work.

Manny has an extraordinarily hard time sitting and focusing. It has gotten increasingly worse as he has gotten older. He isn't diagnosed with anything; his mother is wary of doctors and medication. To accommodate his need for movement and to help him stay focused, he has a standing desk with a leg swing, and a sand timer. He knows his job is to stay focused for ten-minute increments—he has built up to this over the past two months from where he started—two minutes. Alyssa sees his delay in opening his book and starting the timer, so she walks over and says, "Manny, take out the same book you were reading yesterday, open to where you left your bookmark, and start your timer." Looking him directly in the eyes she asks, "Got it?"

"Got it." He answers.

"Remind me of what you are going to do when your timer runs out."

"I'm going to go to the water fountain for a drink, and then I'll work for another ten minutes."

"Right—use your checklist to check off each job you complete. You should have two reading periods and one water break checked off by the time we are done, correct?" She asks with a smile and a hand on the shoulder.

"Correct," he says, and he gets to work.

Scanning the class again, she notes several students at one of the tables who are whispering and have not begun working yet. Otherwise, everyone looks hard at work.

"Green table, books are open, notebooks are open, now," she says in a matter-of-fact tone. One student at the green table, Samari, acts exasperated, pushing her supplies away and throwing her head back. Alyssa knows that Samari's behavior can escalate quickly and become very disruptive to the class, but also knows that too much confrontation with Samari will backfire, so she drops to her knees to get on eye level with Samari and says only for Samari's ears, "I've seen you make better choices. I'm going to give you a minute to make a better choice now. I'll check back in. I know you can do this."

She watches Samari from the corner of her eye but speaks briskly and with precision to the rest of the class, "Class, nice work getting started—you have all of your materials out and I can see how focused you are. You have exactly twenty-four minutes to work. It should remain this quiet and focused the whole time, and you should have at least four boxes on your notebook page filled in that time. We'll share those at the end of reading. I'm going to start conferring, so I want to remind you that unless there is a serious emergency, you are not to interrupt conferences. You all know how to take care of yourselves, each other, and your work for the next twenty-four minutes. If you forgot what your reading job is, the chart that will help you is still on the chart stand." By the time she is finished speaking, Samari is also on task. She makes eye contact with Samari, giving her a wink and a thumbs-up. Samari winks back.

Like most classrooms, Alyssa's has a number of students who require more work and planning than others. She accepts this as a given. There are no point systems in her classrooms, no demerits, no marble jars, and it is a rare occasion when students get sent out. But she does know her students and their needs well, and makes adjusted plans for her students as she sees necessary. She modifies her use of authority in ways she believes will best support her students. To some, Alyssa's interactions may feel overly directed, but she knows these particular students need it. She sets safe boundaries by giving *constructive* attention to help develop students' self-awareness, rather than allowing them to replicate past experiences, where attention was negative and did little to help them build their knowledge of themselves. In doing this, she is helping students develop agency. And remember, there are twenty-three other children in the class who required very little direction—these students were already at the point of self-management with minimal input from Alyssa, because she has explicitly taught them those skills.

From this brief scene, we can tell that Alyssa has made plans with children in their best interests, and we can assume that part of why her students listen to her is both because they have a positive relationship with her and because she has proven she is out for their success. If you have taught for any length of time, though, you know that there are many students who will not simply "allow" you to have authority because you are the teacher—you actually have to work for it—and Alyssa has done that. Authority for teachers is not simply hierarchical but flexible, ever changing, and responsive.

As well, boundaries change, or at least become harder to identify, as students develop internal controls. I remember a group of second graders I taught. Their teacher had left midyear, and they had developed some unproductive habits. For example, during independent reading, they behaved like popping popcorn—getting up to blow a nose, get water, go to the bathroom, sharpen a pencil, pick up a piece of paper off of the floor, swat a fly that was halfway across the classroom—anything but sitting and reading. So I established a very clear boundary. To start, for fifteen minutes of independent reading, they were expected to sit and read—no getting up whatsoever. At first, I sounded like a broken record. "Back in your seat!" 'Back in your seat." Back in your seat!" This was a huge mindset shift for students, but they were so in the habit of acting and reacting without intention that I had to come across as meaning business. It didn't take long for them to behave more intentionally, and with the intention, they started to feel calm and productive.

Not far at all down the road, we had worked to thirty minutes of independent reading with no disruptions, no getting out of seats. Once I knew they had internalized that independent reading time was actually for reading, my boundaries changed. Students were allowed to independently manage when they needed tissues. They no longer needed to ask to go to the bathroom or even move a clothespin to indicate they were at the bathroom. I knew they wouldn't get up to swat a fly on the other side of the classroom. And I was able to sit down and work with students in small groups or one-on-one and not worry about the others.

Similarly, if we fast-forwarded to three months later in Alyssa's classroom, as students have learned to self-manage even more so, her use of authority to influence will have become much more subtle, as students will need less direction. Her boundaries will have evolved. Just as with academic instruction, with classroom management she is using a model of gradual release of responsibility. The teacher begins with a high level of control and gradually releases that control to students, with explicit instruction and practice.

How do you think Alyssa's actions made her students feel? What do you think Samari, Xavier, and Manny would say? What if I told you that I asked them? The students described Alyssa in the following terms:

- "She's a good teacher. A really good teacher."
- "She helps me understand how I can get my work done."
- "She helps me be a better friend to my classmates."
- "She always checks in with you. Like, about how your brother is or your mom or your weekend."
- "She helps me find books I like."
- "She lets me choose where to sit at lunch and writing."
- "She's funny a lot of the time, but she don't play when it comes to class work."
- "She's fair."
- "She never just makes you do things without you knowing why."
- "She never gets on you for no reason like some other teachers do."

It is not surprising that these third graders notice and appreciate that Alyssa has set clear boundaries for them and that she holds them accountable for their work and behavior—in fact, they equate that with her being a good teacher. Fortunately, there are very clear actions you too can take.

How to Communicate Emotional Objectivity

In too many classrooms, I see teachers speaking to students with uncertainty and anxiety, or with anger and frustration. This results in students mirroring those same emotions. For students to feel safe and confident, they need teachers to project safety and confidence, even when they aren't feeling it. The table in Figure 3–4 isn't meant to be used like a script—that would make me as uncomfortable as I am sure it would make many of you. It is meant to be used flexibly and responsively (like Alyssa used it). It is meant to help teachers think about and apply communication tools that will help them project confidence in their interactions with students.

When we enter into a teaching situation with planned and intentional strategies for communication, it helps us keep a healthy emotional distance in situations where we may get frustrated. For example, there were times in my teaching experience where Samari's response to Alyssa might have really frustrated me, and without really thinking about the consequences, I might have gotten into a power struggle with Samari. But with a response that is both planned (meaning, this is in my toolbox and I use it to de-escalate a student's behavior) and responsive to Samari's particular personality and needs, Alyssa creates distance between emotion and action.

After reading the chart in Figure 3–4, reread Alyssa's scenario and see which factors she was using in to establish boundaries.

Extending Emotional Objectivity to Teachers

Paul is a fourth-grade teacher at a "tough" urban school, and because of that, he has many assumptions about how students learn. The reality is, like all other children, the students at this school learn from instruction that is clear and specific, instruction that is adjusted to meet their needs and interests. They learn best when they have choices, and they learn best when they understand the boundaries and are kept safe.

Until Paul's arrival, his students had never received classroom instruction in social skills. They have been controlled, or at least that's what the adults tried to do to them. Their own classroom management experiences had been pieced together and hairy at best, ranging from rewards and consequences to authoritarian. Lots of yelling, lots of marble jars. To say the least, teaching students

Technique	Explanation
Brief sentences for clarity	Speaking in brief sentences with a clear beginning and a clear end. For example, "Kenyon, sit down now." Sentences should not be questions or suggestions, because those imply there are options for students to choose from in responding. Instead, direct commands make clear to the student precisely what needs to be done.
Pacing for emphasis	Pacing should vary to keep the listeners' interest, but when giving a direct command, pacing can allow the command to stand apart from the rest of speech. For example, consider the emphasis created by giving a single command slowly: "Sit . . . down . . . now." Also consider the urgency created when a series of commands are delivered at a brisk pace—imagine this delivered with high energy: "Stand up, push your chairs in, turn your voices off, and move to your line spots."
Firm tone	Tone is a consciously applied inflection of emotion. It is not accidental and does not need to reflect actual emotion. The teacher is always monitoring herself for whether her tone matches her intention. Tone, when giving directions, should sound different than tone when giving praise. Tone when giving directions must communicate "I mean business."
Controlled volume	Volume, like pacing, should vary to keep the listeners' interest and help learners distinguish meaning. Imagine you are going to give a set of directions that are so critically important you want the class to lean in and listen—deliver them at a volume close to a whisper.
Proximity	Especially with directions to individual students or students who are exhibiting the potential for misbehavior, get close when giving directions.
Eye contact	As well, make eye contact when giving directions. Hold the students in your gaze until at least they have begun to show an appropriate response.
Gestures	Gestures are yet another means of communicating meaning. Consider hands clapped together when communicating the direction "quickly" or palm raised to the ceiling to communicate "stand up."

Figure 3–4. Communication Techniques for Emotional Objectivity

responsible independence had not been the focus of instruction. This was a high-needs classroom management class, not for the fainthearted. Not for the teacher without emotional objectivity. But unfortunately for both Paul and his students, he lacked just that.

At the end of the school day, he was crying (maybe the eighth or ninth time I'd seen him cry in the few weeks since school had begun). He shared that his students "just don't care" and "say such mean things" to him. I have worked with some at-risk students who lived through so much trauma that I was in awe of their resolve, of their ability to go on. Because of this, I was disappointed in Paul's reason for crying. Like adults who work in schools, children come to school with a laundry load of issues we can't imagine, and they don't have the tools to process and articulate those issues to get support. It does everyone a disservice to assume that their behaviors can be chalked up to them being mean to us.

I talk to coaches all the time who, like me, get triggered by teacher responses to students. But just like teachers, coaches need to demonstrate emotional objectivity and need to provide support. So I remind myself and I remind coaches in situations like this to create emotional distance—if this is where Paul is at, I can't hold him hostage for not being like me—my job is to figure out how to help him. I have to start by getting Paul, and teachers like him, to think about the outcomes that they want for their students and their classrooms. Then, we can start designing a path that not only will get them there but will fit with who they are as people.

Over the years, I have developed at least a few tools that can help remind teachers like Paul to have some emotional distance between him, the professional, and the children he is teaching. These tools also serve as reminders to me (and other coaches I have coached) when I am in a coaching position.

The single most important thing to help teachers keep in mind when things get heated is that the issue, the problem, the interaction, is a professional one in which the teacher must focus on adjusting the student's *behavior*. All too often teachers get caught up in seeing students being fixed beings (as we sometimes see teachers as fixed beings), and then things get personal—me versus them. But behavior is never fixed. Behavior can always change. So I share with teachers my own technique in challenging situations with students—I've given myself a "tagline" to use to remind myself that I must focus on the behavior, not the child.

I learned to use this technique with my own son, when I felt myself getting heated. He went through a phase where he would turn a minor correction (and there were lots of them) into a "Nobody likes me! That's why I'm always in trouble," which would really push my buttons.

But somewhere along the way, I planned to try something different and was ready with a new response. The next time he said that I didn't like him and that he was in trouble, I said, "Do you think you are in trouble? You're not in trouble. But your behavior needs to change." A simple, canned response like that diffused the me-versus-you issue and focused me and him on the behavior and allowed my stress hormones to stay low. Not only did it create distance, but I gained control, and as a result, so did he. I use lines like that all the time in classrooms when I see a conflict brewing, and I coach teachers through similar situations with similar responses. I help teachers plan for a different response to a repeated behavior, especially one that has triggered them—that right there is emotional objectivity in practice.

For Paul, a new teacher, establishing boundaries was of critical importance for him to manage his class both safely and effectively, but it was a great struggle for him. He couldn't understand what was going wrong. He was certain he was exerting authority but for some reason the students were not listening. If he wasn't exerting authority, then he couldn't imagine what it was supposed to look like.

Early in the school year, I demonstrated lessons for Paul and asked him to use the tool below to focus his observations. Next, I videotaped Paul and asked him to watch himself using the tools above. There's an objective distance with video viewing that can help the learning process. This exercise brought Paul to an "aha!" moment, when he recognized what teaching with authority and establishing boundaries really looked like and that he himself hadn't been doing it.

Sentence Length and Type	
What It Should Sound Like	Speak in brief sentences with a clear beginning and a clear end. For example, "Kenyon, sit down now." Sentences should not be questions or suggestions but rather direct commands.
What Paul Observes in His Teaching	If I saw my sentences in writing, they'd be run-on sentences. There's no clear break and a number of directions are strung together. I do lots of explaining about each direction and why students need to listen to them. It almost sounds like pleading.

Pacing	
What It Should Sound Like	Pacing changes so that emphasis changes. So when transitions are supposed to be done quickly, directions are delivered quickly. During instruction, the pace is much slower. The pauses extend between sentences. Students are allowed time to process more deeply. For example, consider the emphasis created by giving a single command slowly: "Sit . . . down . . . now." Also consider the urgency created when a series of commands are delivered at a brisk pace—imagine this delivered with high energy: "Stand up, push your chairs in, turn your voices off, and move to your line spots."
What Paul Observes in His Teaching	Everything is the same pace, quick, quick, quick, with one sentence rolling into the next.

Tone	
What It Should Sound Like	When teaching with authority, tone is a consciously applied inflection of emotion. It is not accidental and does not need to reflect actual emotion. Tone, when giving directions, should sound different than tone when giving praise. It must communicate "I mean business." During academic instruction, it is hard to capture, but it sounds somewhat intense and energetic, like she is communicating the most important message on earth.
What Paul Observes in His Teaching	Tone is always the same, whether I am giving praise or correcting behavior. There are slight changes, but they are barely perceptible.

Volume	
What It Should Sound Like	Volume, like pacing, should vary to keep the listener's interest and help learners distinguish meaning. Imagine you are going to give a set of directions that are so critically important you want the class to lean in and listen—deliver them at a volume close to a whisper. Academic instruction is at a normal conversational volume.
What Paul Observes in His Teaching	As with tone, there is very little variation in tone. However, it is obvious that I get louder when I am feeling frustrated.

Proximity	
What It Should Look Like	Even during direct instruction, the teacher sits, stands, kneels, moves—always close to students, but still dynamic. During independent work, teacher gently and briefly lays a hand on a shoulder to quiet a student, kneels down to whisper to a student.
What Paul Observes in His Teaching	No evidence of using proximity. During instruction I am glued to my seat, and when students are at tables, I am generally standing too far for any contact to occur.

Eye Contact	
What It Should Look Like	During instruction and while giving directions, scan the room, constantly connecting through eye contact with each student. When giving directions to individual students, hold eye contact the entire time and keeps your eyes there until they follow the direction.
What Paul Observes in His Teaching	I make eye contact with some students but not all. When I give directions to individual students, I often look away mid-delivery.

Gestures	
What It Should Look Like	Gestures are yet another means of communicating meaning. Consider hands clapped together when communicating the direction "quickly," or palm raised to the ceiling to communicate "stand up." Use facial gestures to reflect the meaning of what you're saying—smiles with praise, looks stern with redirection. Use hands—for example, claps them together when praising with a "Yes!" Gestures increase attention.
What Paul Observes in His Teaching	I rarely smile or look particularly stern—my facial gestures are hard to discern. Sometimes I point where I want students to look, but generally, there's little change in how I look.

Did this aha! result in a quick turnaround for Paul? No, but it was the beginning of a turnaround. The first step to changing practice is the recognition of the need, and the second step is seeing and believing that there are tools. Through this exercise, he took both steps.

REFLECTION   How Can I Evaluate My Emotional Objectivity?

Whether or not you feel like you are struggling with establishing boundaries, perhaps you can use a similar process to reflect on the boundaries you mean to have established and the progress you have made. Can you assess your practice to determine what your needs are? And if so, what will you use that you learned here as tools for change? Using the same table Paul used, videotape yourself, or have a colleague watch you. Use Figure 3–5.

It's powerful to use a tool like this as part of a reflection and goal-setting process. I recently did this myself. I didn't need to watch a video to know that I come across as "intense" as a teacher. So in watching, I saw that I needed to show children more moments of levity so that my intensity would carry greater meaning. So after a first video, I decided to consciously smile more, have moments of chipper feedback to students when they did something well, and use some playful hand gestures—a high five, fist bump, and so on. After the second viewing, I could see that although I felt much more lighthearted while teaching, what I looked like didn't quite match my intention. So the next time, I built some check points into my lesson plan where I could remind myself to adjust my communication. This process took a bit of time to work through, but once I felt like I met my small goal, I gave myself some space. I try to check in on myself every three or four months through a video, and if more is needed, I'll use this process again.

Be sure to use a process and timeline that works for you. Don't set your sights on a complete overhaul of your communication, but set small goals and a timeline for three or four video sessions. Then give yourself some space to try your new tools before reflecting again.

Ways We Communicate	What I Notice About How I Communicate (in One Lesson/ Stretch of Time)
Sentence length and type	
Pacing	
Tone	
Volume	
Proximity	
Eye contact	
Gestures	

Figure 3–5. Evaluate Communication of Emotions During Instruction

4

Why Do Children Misbehave and How Should I Respond?

Almost anything can become a learning experience if there is enough caring involved.

—MARY MacCRACKEN

I'm sure you've all seen children with pants that no longer even reach their ankles, or the ghost of a toe poking against their sneakers, and the child complaining, "These are too tight!" Growth pushing against something trying to contain it causes discomfort. Children moving from one stage of development and understanding to another are bound to create some degree of disruption. Even when we are proactive and emotionally supportive, children misbehave. This is perfectly natural.

The longer I work with children, the more I realize the ways we respond to children's misbehavior are not clear-cut. Because children are in different places in their social and emotional learning, there's no one way to respond, no regimented ladder of discipline to follow. There is more than one good way to be a teacher and more than one good way to respond to behavioral issues.

Too often our responses are based on what a child's behavior *is* rather than why he may be acting the way he does. When we limit our response to the behavior, we follow the path taken by our criminal justice system: we punish without understanding. We communicate that there is no room in our culture for bad behavior. We banish the misbehaver from the community—in the case of children, from the very community that could and should be teaching the necessary alternative behavior skills. Punishment doesn't teach children how to behave and may instead communicate that they are not competent, not part of the community.

Our responses to disruption are often ineffective because we do not understand from what the misbehavior stems. Knowing the reasons children misbehave can make our responses more reasonable and caring. There is always a reason, and we can't solve the problem without knowing what that reason is.

The Cause for Misbehavior Matters

Human beings share three fundamental needs: relatedness, competence, and autonomy (Connell and Wellborn 1991; Deci et al. 1991). When these needs are not met, children are likely to misbehave. Students are more apt to behave negatively when they do not feel cared for by the teacher and/or their peers and therefore lack a sense of relatedness (Roorda et al. 2011). Students may misbehave when they do not feel academically competent and/or when they do not have any control over activities in the classroom (Kern and Clemens 2007). When tasks are too difficult for them, they may misbehave to avoid the work (Bohn, Roehring, and Pressley 2004; Center, Deitz, and Kaufman 1982; Mayer 1995). They may also misbehave when they don't view the work as challenging enough to further their competence

Children's behavior is also influenced by family and societal factors. Negative behavior is related to living in poverty or in violent communities, family stress, family conflict, family structure (single-parent homes, for example), family instability (separation/divorce, relocation, homelessness), harsh parenting/maltreatment, maternal depression, and malnourishment (Ackerman, Brown, and Izard 2004; Conroy and Brown 2004; Fauth, Roth, and Brooks-Gunn 2007; Qi and Kaiser 2003; Waldfogel, Craigie, and Brooks-Gunn 2010). There is a striking disproportion between the number of ethnic minority children and white children who live in poverty: 34 percent of black children, 27 percent of Hispanic children, and 10 percent of white children (National Center for Education Statistics [NCES] 2010).

Some behavior that we are inclined to label misbehavior may be developmentally and/or culturally appropriate. Young boys are more likely to be physically active, impulsive, and dysregulated, quicker to express frustrations and anger, than girls (Else-Quest et al. 2006; Zahn-Waxler, Shiftcliff, and Marceau 2008). Children from different cultures may experience a mismatch between what is considered appropriate behavior at home and at school. Thompson (2007) describes how African American students' normal loud and outspoken speaking style can be interpreted by teachers as being defiant and questioning authority. Behavior needs to be interpreted in culturally responsive ways. We need to learn the norms of children's behavior in various contexts—schools, homes, communities. Behavior different from that expected and valued in schools may serve children well in other situations (Lareau 2011). We must not take a deficit view of children, families, and communities. (Many of the educators' statements quoted in the introduction are examples of deficit-based thinking: "This type of instruction doesn't work for these kids," for example.)

As teachers, we serve our children (and ourselves) best when we take a strengths-based approach. It is appropriate to teach children alternate ways of behaving that will serve them well in schools and similar institutions/settings, but we can do this in a way that supplements their existing knowledge while still valuing the strengths and unique qualities they bring to the classroom.

Students typically misbehave either to get or to avoid something (Epstein et al. 2008). To provide effective interventions that help children function in the classroom, we need to know why students misbehave (Bambara and Knoster 2009; Epstein et al. 2008). The initial step is to identify what behavioral analysts call the *antecedents* and *consequences* of the behavior (Bambara and Knoster 2009; Epstein et al. 2008). An *antecedent* is what is happening immediately prior to the misbehavior; a *consequence* is what occurs immediately after the student misbehaves. Consider this scenario: As math class begins (antecedent), Sebastian talks incessantly to his classmates (behavior), distracting them and himself from the lesson; as a result he is sent to time-out in another teacher's classroom (consequence). His teacher is in essence reinforcing Sebastian's misbehavior by allowing him to avoid math instruction, a subject he finds difficult. So, what do we do instead? Let's look at the research.

When Misbehavior Occurs, Offer a Positive Choice

As teachers, our emphasis should be on developing positive behavior, not on elim-inating the undesirable behavior (Mayer 1995). Hojnoski, Gischlar, and Missall (2009) call this the *fair-pair rule*: pairing a desirable behavior with the undesirable behavior. Sebastian's unwanted behavior is incessant talking; suggesting the desir-able behavior of keeping his eyes on the teacher during the lesson switches the behavioral focus to the positive—reinforcing Sebastian for focusing on the teacher rather than punishing him for talking.

We need to ask ourselves some key questions regarding the desired behav-ior (Umbreit et al. 2007; Wood and Ferro 2014). Does the child currently have the skills to perform it? Do we need to adjust our classroom environment and/or instruction to elicit it? Based on our responses, we decide how to modify the class-room environment/instruction and/or teach the child necessary skills.

We also have to identify a reward and reward schedule that will lead to an initial and sustained increase in the wanted behavior (Mayer 1995). The reward tells the child that she successfully exhibited the desirable behavior (Reeve 2006). It's not something with which to coerce or bribe the student ("You do that, you get this") but a way to communicate that you saw him engage in the desired behavior ("Sebastian, I saw that you began your math work without talking; you earned five minutes of extra recess today"). How rewards or reinforcements are given should change as the child gains more competence (Akin-Little et al. 2004; Rhode, Jenson, and Reavis 1993). For example, Sebastian may initially be rewarded for every ten minutes he is able to focus on the lesson. As his stamina increases, his reward may systematically decrease to once a math lesson to one or two times a week to once a month.

Sometimes a student's behavior will initially *worsen*, something referred to as a "rebound effect" (Epstein et al. 2008). Epstein and colleagues recommend con-tinuing to follow a behavior plan for at least month.

How to Respond to Misbehavior: A Change-Over-Time Approach

The antecedent–behavior–consequence (ABC) approach has been used by behav-ior specialists, special educators, and classroom teachers for years. The premise is simple. Antecedents help us determine the motivations for student behavior.

Understanding motivations helps us see the consequences the child wants, which can usually be tied to basic human needs—getting attention even if it is negative, getting sent out of class so she doesn't have to do math. Knowing what consequence the child is seeking helps us determine more effective supports as well as consequences. (A *consequence* is not synonymous with *punishment*. It is something that happens as a result of something that occurred earlier.)

Let's examine a case study in which a student's teachers and I analyze his behavior using the ABC method (which should really be called the BCA method, because we always start with the student's behavior, look at the consequences next, then the antecedents) and introduce a fair-pair intervention strategy, in which a negative behavior is replaced with a positive one.

Jaleel lives with his mom and his older brother, who is eleven. Dad has been in prison for four years, and Mom works the evening custodial shift at a high school. A grandfather is in and out of the picture. Jaleel and his brother ride the school bus home and feed themselves (with food in the cupboard and the refrigerator if there is any, but often relying on bags filled with lunchroom leftovers). They manage their own nightly routine, often playing in the streets until late. Mom is home in the morning and gets them up and back on the school bus.

Jaleel often comes to school hungry; his teachers know this and have breakfast waiting. He exchanges hearty hugs with many adults on the way to the classroom. Since kindergarten, his behavioral issues have been the same. He is impulsive and blurts out comments incessantly, usually things disconnected from the class lesson ("Dylan is picking his nose!" "Everybody look, it's snowing outside!" "I've got to go to the bathroom!"). His teachers are frustrated and don't know how to get him to stop. If he gets a response—if Dylan is angry at being told on, for example—getting Jaleel to disengage is nearly impossible; the verbal exchange seems to be what he wants.

He is often "handsy" as well, lots of touching of other kids, which they interpret as bullying. Comments like "Dylan is picking his nose" don't help him form friendships, either. In reading, he is in the bottom third of his class; in math, he is in the upper third. Everyone knows Jaleel, and he has a smiling response to everything—even getting into trouble. For the most part, teachers "manage" him by keeping him separate from the rest of the class, which seems to be the one thing, at least initially, that makes him angry. He spends part of the day doing independent work in a former teacher's room, an arrangement he increasingly resists.

Tanya, a school social worker, has been observing Jakeel (see Figure 4–1).

ABC Problem-Solving Guide		
[A]ntecedent	**[B]ehavior**	**[C]onsequence**
Use antecedents to help you determine the motivation for student behavior. Understanding motivation helps you determine more effective consequences. » When does the behavior occur? » What is the child doing? » Who is the child near? » What is the difficulty of the task? » Is there a pattern? » Is there anything else going on that can help you determine a possible motivation for the behavior?	Define the behavior in precise language. » What does the child say and do that is problematic?	Determine whether the consequences that follow a behavior are the right ones. For example, if a child is motivated by the desire to avoid math, sending him to the office when he misbehaves during a math lesson is the wrong consequence. » What happens as a result of the behavior?
When the class moves from classroom tables to the meeting-area carpet, each child has an assigned "square" on which to sit, but Jaleel has to sit on a chair behind the group.	Jaleel rocks back and forth in his seat, making faces at other children.	Jaleel gets the attention of his classmates and Teri, who warns him that his behavior is not okay.
Teri, Jaleel's teacher, begins preparing the students for recess, reminding them to bundle up because it is cold outside.	Jaleel yells, "Let's see if it's cold outside!" and runs to look out the window, waving others over to join him.	Jaleel receives more attention—giggling from classmates and another redirection from Teri to return to his seat immediately.
Students review the steps for putting their work away before recess.	Jaleel gets up, goes to his cubby to look for something, and then loudly says, "I have an extra notebook!"	Student attention is on Jaleel, and he is all smiles.

Figure 4–1. ABC Problem-Solving Guide

I meet with Tanya and his classroom teacher, Teri, to discuss next steps. We agree that Jaleel has the most trouble during transitions (which are long) and carpet activities (which are also long). At both times, he is separate from the group, his role is unclear, but his desire to interact with the group (even if negatively) is strong. His blurted comments disrupt his relationship with Teri and his peers. However, Jaleel is getting the consequence he wants: attention.

We all agree it is important for Jaleel to get attention, but we want to shift this attention from negative to positive while also helping him restrain his blurted comments. We also acknowledge that while we'd like the shift in Jaleel's behavior to happen quickly, that's an unfair expectation and sets him up to fail. It will take between four and eight weeks at a minimum to see evidence that our plan is working, and then only if it is implemented consistently. It could be a year before the change is really significant. Realistically, we are looking for improvement over time, not a completely different child next week.

Next we meet with Jaleel to get his take on what is going on. I tell him briefly what we have noticed, and he nods and smiles. (He almost always smiles.) I ask him why he blurts out comments. "I have lot I want to say about the lesson," he says (again with that smile).

"Really, because what I hear you saying isn't about the lesson. Here are some things you said today." I read them to him.

"Oh yeah. I think I just want to talk to my friends." Ah. I need to remember that.

I remind Jaleel what happens as a result of his behavior—working in another teacher's room, time-outs, sitting separately, redirections. He is very clear that he doesn't like these things and doesn't want to leave the room anymore. He says he wants to work with children who make good decisions and who can help him.

"Who is that?" I ask.

"Alena," he responds immediately.

Alena has excellent impulse control and is generally very responsible, exhibiting a good balance of getting along with everyone while being assertive when necessary. Jaleel suggests that Alena become his carpet partner during working and sharing sessions.

"And can you watch her to figure out what your job is on the carpet and during transitions?" He readily agrees. We decide on a signal Teri can use to tell him to look at Alena and correct his behavior.

"What else do you need?" I ask.

"Something in my hands," he answers.

It's true. If nothing is in his hands, he'll find something and it will be the wrong thing. He asks for a squishy ball. (Sidebar: During day one, he hurls it at classmates many times. The squishy ball is history, and we decide on a notebook, in which he can take notes or doodle, as long as the notebook and pen stay in his hands. He thinks that when he gets the urge to call out a comment, he can scribble something instead.)

"Anything else?"

There is. At recess and lunch and during choice activities, he wants to choose his friends like everyone else gets to, not be told where to sit and what to play. He names several students he will choose to be around.

"How will you know if you are doing a good job?" I ask.

"My teacher should tell me."

We tell Jaleel we will get back to him and outline the plan in Figure 4–2, first making sure Alena is comfortable with her role. (For behavior plans to be effective, they have to be implemented faithfully, carefully, and patiently. There's no quick fix to changing student behavior.)

Always remember that for behavior plans to be effective, they have to be implemented with fidelity, care, and with patience. There's no quick fix to changing student behavior.

REFLECTION How Can Inquiry Inform My Response to Misbehavior?

Now you try it. Think of a student in your class whose negative behavior stands out. You've tried different approaches but haven't been successful. Observe the student and answer the questions in Figure 4–3, and have a colleague do so as well. Sit down with your colleague and compare your observations; then create a fair-pair plan together (see Figure 4–4).

The most important thing to remember is that change takes time and occurs in small steps. Jaleel didn't stop calling out comments completely. Change began when replacement behavior led to fewer instances of the misbehavior. Don't expect a "cured" student after a week; you'll be disappointed, and your student will

The Fair-Pair Plan

Targeted behavior(s):

Blurting out comments during carpet activities.

Replacement behavior(s):

When Jaleel feels he needs/is about to call something out, he will draw/write in notebook. He will have his notebook with him in the carpet area at all times.

Does the child currently have the skills to implement replacement behavior(s)? If not, describe the changes in environment, procedure, or instruction that will support implementation of replacement behavior:

Environment:

Jaleel will sit next to Alena on the carpet and stand behind her when students line up before leaving the room. She will model desired behavior. At recess and lunch and during choice activities, he will not be told where to sit and what to play.

Procedure:

» Jaleel will use a notebook during carpet activities as a replacement for blurting comments out loud.
» Teri will model a mentoring relationship for Jaleel and Alena.
» Teri will point to her eyes with two fingers when she wants Jaleel to look at Alena and copy her behavior.

Instruction:

Twice a week Teri will work on social skills with Jaleel and a small group of his choice: Malik, Jordan, Kevin, and Bryan.

Desired frequency of replacement behavior(s):

By week four, Jaleel will use the notebook 20 percent of the time instead of calling out comments. Plan will be updated after four weeks.

Daily reward(s) or reinforcement(s):

» Provide frequent positive oral reinforcement.
» Allow Jaleel to run an errand if he is behaving appropriately, particularly during transitions and unstructured times.
» Have him work with peers of his choice.

Remember:

Rewards are not used to bribe/coerce but to reinforce—not "Remember, if you _____ , then you'll get _____ ," but "I saw you _____ , so now _____ ."

Assessment:

Teri will record the number of times Jaleel calls out comments during carpet activities. We will review his progress at four-week intervals.

Figure 4–2. The Fair-Pair Plan

Student:		
Observed by:		
[A]ntecedent	**[B]ehavior**	**[C]onsequence**
Use antecedents to help you determine the motivation for student behavior. Understanding motivation helps you determine more effective consequences.	Define the behavior in precise language. » What does the child say and do that is problematic?	Determine whether the consequences that follow a behavior are the right ones. For example, if a child is motivated by the desire to avoid math, sending him to the office when he misbehaves during a math lesson is the wrong consequence.
» When does the behavior occur? » What is the child doing? » Who is the child near? » What is the difficulty of the task? » Is there a pattern? » Is there anything else going on that can help you determine a possible motivation for the behavior?		» What happens as a result of the behavior?

Figure 4–3. Problem-Solve Behavior

feel incompetent. Do expect small changes that grow over time as old habits are replaced with new ones. And be sure your student knows just how huge a success that is. You don't have to be the only vehicle for information. In the next section, you'll read the research on peer feedback.

Formalizing Peer Feedback

We are influenced by the behavior of those around us (Bandura 1965); they are models for how we conduct ourselves. This is also true for children. Peers can positively (the good news) and negatively (the bad news) influence children's behavior (Richards, Heathfield, and Jenson 2010; Stearns, Dodge, and Nicholson 2008). For example, Boxer and colleagues (2005) found that aggressive third graders who

The Fair-Pair Plan
Targeted behavior(s):
Replacement behavior(s):
Does the child currently have the skills to implement replacement behavior(s)? If not, describe the changes in environment, procedure, or instruction that will support implementation of replacement behavior: Environment: Procedure: Instruction:
Desired frequency of replacement behavior(s): **Remember:**
Daily reward(s) or reinforcement(s):
Assessment:

Figure 4–4. The Fair-Pair Plan

interact with less (versus more) aggressive peers decreased their level of aggressive behavior. Children, like adults, are most likely to be influenced by peers who are similar to themselves or that are important to them (Dishion, Poulin, and Burraston 2001). Gender is one influential factor (Maccoby 2004). Stearns and colleagues (2008) found that boys exacted more influence on other boys' behavior, and girls were more influential as models to other girls.

We can formalize opportunities for children to exercise their influence for their own good and the good of others. I'll share an example.

Martin often lost his temper in Erika's fourth-grade class. He'd interrupt the class, get sent to a time-out seat, and, in frustration, kick a child on his way there. If he arrived at a spot in line at the same time as a classmate, he'd angrily push him or her out of the way for "skipping" him.

His classmates were upset—perhaps more deeply than we adults initially realized. One boy stopped me in the hall and asked, "Why does Martin get to treat us that way and get to come back to class?" Martin had been suspended before, but research shows that suspension leads to suspension, not acquisition of social competence. It was time we helped the students assert themselves as part of an effort to help Martin develop self-awareness and, we hoped, a greater ability to regulate his behavior. I spoke with Erika's class without Martin there, while another teacher prepared Martin for what was coming.

"I know you are upset with Martin's recent behavior and that some of you are worried about him being in your class." There were lots of vigorous nods of agreement and even a few tears. "You have every right to be upset about the way he has treated you. It is not okay. You may not know this, but you all have lots of power you can use to help Martin know that the way he has been acting isn't good for this community and that you need him to be different. You can help him be different! Martin is part of this community—he isn't going anywhere—so I'm going to help you help him, and at the same time, I'm going to help you begin to get what you need from him so that you feel taken care of and safe. This isn't going to be a quick fix, but you can help him become aware of his behavior so he can begin to change. You're going to start by practicing with me."

I asked the students to tell me, as if I were Martin, as directly and respectfully as possible, how his actions made them feel and what they needed from him to feel better. We talked about how hard it is to change patterns or habits of behavior and that they shouldn't have unrealistic expectations for Martin's improvement. I suggested they speak in a way that allowed Martin to truly hear, which included making sure Martin knew they liked him but not his behavior. We also discussed asking Martin what he needs from his peers. It took only a little coaching—the students were amazingly succinct, respectful, and articulate on the first try:

- "I love how hard you play when we are playing basketball, and you are so good at passing and shooting. But I don't like when you act angry. It makes me feel scared, like you might hurt me."
- "When you are calm and happy, you are a good classmate. When you get mad, I get nervous and I can't learn. I need you to promise you will try hard not to act that way anymore."
- "Sometimes you are so funny and you tell great jokes. But then, I'm never sure what will make you angry. It makes me not want to be around you, because I am worried that something I will do will make you mad."
- "We know you might get angry again, everybody gets angry, and it is okay. But you need to find somewhere to go away from us when you feel yourself getting upset. You can't shove or kick us anymore when you get upset."
- "Tell us what you need from us. We care about you and will help you get this done."
- "You need to tell us if you understand what we are saying. That will help us trust you again."

They were ready to talk to Martin.

Martin, however, wasn't ready to listen. He broke down in tears when he found out his classmates wanted him to know how upset they were. Developing self-awareness can be a scary experience, and Martin was afraid to hear what his classmates thought of him. When she receives feedback from an adult, a child can easily assume it's just this person who has a problem with her. But there is nowhere to hide from peer feedback.

It took a full day before Martin would enter the classroom. One courageous classmate spoke to Martin alone in another room to give him some practice at hearing the feedback and to let him know the students were not going to attack him or disrespect him—they just needed him to know how they felt and to behave in a way that allowed them to feel safe. When Martin finally heard from the class, he was ready to listen with an open mind and heart and to respond sincerely when he apologized.

No one expects Martin never to act out again—we all make the same mistakes again and again and again. Change takes time. However, this experience opened the door for Martin to really understand where he stood with others and, as important, empowered his classmates to assert themselves and establish clear boundaries to keep themselves safe. They were able to effect change for themselves and for Martin.

A word of caution: All parties, including the student who has "wronged" others, must be protected and feel safe. Unless skillfully handled, this approach can easily be perceived as an attack on the child. But it works well in an established, caring community and can be powerful under the right conditions.

Suspensions Don't Work—and Aren't Fair

Often in situations like Martin's, especially when the child's classmates tell their parents they are afraid, the parents demand the child be suspended and, if he isn't, believe nothing was done to resolve the situation or support the students. This speaks to the culture we live in—our crime-and-punishment mentality. School suspensions are a common consequence for misbehavior (Allman and State 2011; Chin et al. 2012), especially in schools with zero tolerance policies. I'll say it plainly and simply: suspensions (or other exclusionary disciplinary practices) do not change behavior (American Psychological Association [APA] 2008). No matter how we've dealt with school discipline in the past and no matter how our society functions, research shows that punishment is an ineffective way to respond to children's misbehavior.

We know this for a variety of reasons. First, students are often suspended repeatedly (Chin et al. 2012), which tells us that suspensions are not an effective way to reduce challenging behavior. Second, research has shown that children need to be explicitly taught behavioral expectations and have the opportunity to practice using more positive behavior. Students who are removed from their classrooms miss the opportunity both to be taught behavioral expectations and to practice these new skills. In addition, being removed from school for a prolonged period leads students to fall behind academically and disengage (Allman and State 2011; Chin et al. 2012; Hemphill and Hargreaves 2009). Feelings of competence and relatedness are important factors in students' behavior (Roorda et al. 2011).

Suspension statistics indicate that certain groups of students are disproportionately suspended. African American males are much more likely to be suspended than other student groups even when the number of office referrals are the same (Skiba et al. 2011). And whatever the triggering behavior, African American males are twice as likely as white males and black females and six times as likely as white females to be suspended (Gay 2006). Recent statistics published by the National Center for Education Statistics indicates that half of African American males in grades 6–12 have been suspended at least once (NCES 2010). Seventeen percent of African American males are expelled compared with 1 percent of white students, male and female (NCES 2010). Other factors related to higher suspension (and expulsion) rates include a special education classification, low socioeconomic status, and family structure (living in foster care or a single-parent home, for example) (Fantuzzo and Perlman 2007; Hinojosa 2008; Sullivan, Klingbeil, and Van Nortnan 2013).

Students who are suspended are more likely to drop out of high school, which increases the likelihood they will interact with the justice system (APA 2008). Zero tolerance policies also increase the referrals schools make to the juvenile justice system. This phenomenon has been termed the "school-to-prison pipeline" and is a serious concern facing our educational and justice systems.

Nevertheless, there may be times when we feel suspension is a necessary response. I have suspended students in my time as a school leader. Early in my career, I passed the buck: "Students who behave like that don't belong here—this is someone else's problem." But my thinking has evolved. I no longer believe children, troubled or not, are anyone else's problem but that of the adults they live with and learn with. But not all adults who work in schools agree with me, nor do many parents. I base my suspensions on one guiding principle: the staff first needs time to make a plan for the child. Time to use the ABC approach to create a fair-pair plan. Time to change the environment to support the behaviorally challenged student. Time to change the interventions to support the behaviorally challenged student.

Suspensions should be resorted to only if it is unsafe to have the child in the building. These circumstances are rare. Children whom I believe fit this category (and whom I've suspended) include:

- a sixth grader who brought a gun to school
- a seventh grader who held a pair of scissors to another student's neck and threatened to stab her
- a fifth grader who persistently bullied other students using threats and physical intimidation
- a second grader, prone to tantrums, who threw a chair in the classroom and attempted to choke a child at recess.

The greatest injustice related to school suspensions is believing a suspension will change student behavior. It won't. The student most likely to be suspended is the student who needs the greatest amount of caring intervention and support from the school community he or she is a part of.

To not only *be* effective at dealing with disruptive behavior but also *feel* effective, we have to remember that children, like adults, are imperfect and ever changing. Teaching a student to be less physical with others doesn't mean the child will never have another behavioral incident; it's reasonable to expect she will. It doesn't mean she's bad, nor does it mean you've failed. Children need reminders. Some children will need periods of heavy support interspersed with periods of less support. The most important belief to avoid is that once we've supported a student, all problems are resolved and we are done. Although that would make our jobs so much more manageable, it's not how it works.

5

How Can Instruction Help Students Practice and Reflect on Behavior?

Much education today is monumentally ineffective. All too often we are giving young people cut flowers when we should be teaching them to grow their own plants.

—JOHN W. GARDNER, *Self-Renewal: The Individual and the Innovative Society*

She just keeps talking and talking. She goes on forever. Why can't she just let us get to work?" This was the response of a fifth grader when asked why he keeps interrupting during the lesson. He can't, or won't, sit still or keep quiet. But like many other students, he doesn't have a choice in how this lesson goes. He's expected to persevere regardless.

Too often, we fail to examine our instruction from the perspective of those being taught. We're asked to evaluate our teaching in terms of learning targets, standards, assessment, college and career readiness, and so on—but for what and for whose larger purpose? The essential question of instruction—what are those being taught learning?—too often goes unanswered. This means that we don't pay attention to how our instruction affects our students. "Covering curriculum" too often means covering up students' identities: We forget about our relationship with them, their feelings and capability, their self-sufficiency and social and emotional skills. We measure the success of our instruction through those students who succeed: if some students can succeed, those who fail are their own problem.

Here's what that acceptance of limited success really communicates. When we normalize that response through institutionwide expectations that "some students will misbehave; that's not our problem" and "some students won't learn; that's not our problem," we are building a tiered society—the ones who belong and the outsiders. Many children come into our classroom as outsiders, but our response should not be to label them; instead, we must ask ourselves, *how can we invite them in?*

The larger purpose of instruction is an invitation to make meaning. Within the field of education, we balance the needs of individual meaning making with the larger needs of society. The United States can proudly claim a history of forward-thinking educators, from John Dewey to Diane Ravitch and Deb Meier, who argue that society needs education to prepare children to be participants in a democracy. That means, in the most practical terms, that we need to facilitate learning, not deliver it. We need to engage students in a way that connects them to a classroom community that makes them think, wonder, question, and explore, a community in which discussion, disagreement, and debate are not only honored but expected. When students don't feel like the classroom is a safe place to take risks because they don't have a trusting relationship with their teacher or peers, don't have the social competence necessary to engage in the work, are frustrated with the work—it's too boring, too difficult, they simply don't understand—or feel they have no say in what happens, they will often act out as a way of not participating. Many schools and teacher training programs have real difficulty connecting the dots on this topic, so let's look at what the research says.

Our Academic Lives Promote Specific Behaviors

Effective and engaging instruction leads to increased learning and positive student behavior (Bohn, Roehrig, and Pressley 2004). This is not surprising given that optimal instruction supports students' fundamental human needs. That is, instruction provides students with opportunities to be a member of a learning community (relatedness), builds students' skills and self-perceptions (competence), and allows students to make choices and own their learning (autonomy). Specifically, appropriate and engaging instruction means that teachers provide:

- *High expectations.* Bohn, Roehrig, and Pressley (2004) found that effective teachers hold high academic expectations for all their students, whereas ineffective teachers express doubt about some students' ability to do the work. Although effective teachers hold high expectations for all students, they do not hold the *same* expectations for all students.

- *Opportunities for active participation.* Effective teachers provide students with varied opportunities to engage with instruction in ways that support their learning (Kern and Clemens 2007). When students are active participants in their instruction, their learning and competence improves. One simple way to provide students with a voice in their learning is by offering them choices regarding their instruction (Bohn, Roehrig, and Pressley 2004; Kern, Bambara, and Fogt 2002). Choice also supports students' autonomy in the classroom. Providing choice is a good way to connect children's interests and background knowledge to the instructional content (Emmer, Evertson, and Anderson 1980). In turn, students, even those with severe emotional and behavioral disorders, are more engaged and exhibit less problem behavior when they are provided choice (Kern et al. 2002).

- *Varied instructional delivery.* Effective teachers modify the way they deliver their instruction to sustain active student engagement. For instance, some students have very short attention spans. Frequently switching activities, incorporating movement into the lesson or between activities, using a variety of activity structures (whole group, small group, pairs) are ways to sustain student attention (Epstein et al. 2008).

- *Scaffolded support.* Researchers have found that teachers provide misbehaving students with inadequate instructional support (Jones and Bouffard 2012). This is a cyclical problem: Children who misbehave because the academic tasks are not at the correct academic level (Bohn, Roehrig, and Pressley 2004) are the ones who most need instructional support and may be the least likely to receive the appropriate level of instruction for their ability/skill. To identify the appropriate level of instruction, teachers must know their students well and have positive relationships with them.

- *Just-right challenges.* Teachers should differentiate instruction to teach at just the right level of challenge (also known as the *zone of proximal development*) for individual students (Gettinger and Kohler 2006; Pressley et al. 2003). Optimal instruction targets what the child is able to successfully do with support. The task should be more difficult than she can accomplish independently but not so hard that she cannot succeed even with assistance from an adult. In this way, teachers build students' academic competence.

- *Opportunities for social interaction.* According to Vygotsky's social learning theory (1978), we advance our learning by engaging in social interactions with others. More knowledgeable adults and peers advance the learning of children. This is accomplished in the classroom in many ways, including cooperative learning and interactive discussions. In cooperative learning, students work in small groups and jointly engage in activities that share a common goal. Cooperative learning is associated with greater gains in academic achievement *and* social skills. Students are likely to be more engaged, have higher academic achievement, exhibit less problem behavior and more prosocial behavior, and develop a more positive classroom community (Ebrahim 2012; Johnson and Johnson 2004; Kamps et al. 1999; Solomon et al. 2000). Students or teachers can also facilitate rich interactive discussions, sometimes called *collaborative discussions* or *grand conversations*, that promote students' reasoning, language skills, and prosocial skills (Murphy et al. 2009). These discussions give students opportunities to hear others' perspectives, respond in respectful and thoughtful manners, and articulate their own points of view.

How to Create Instruction That Develops the Learner

How might these instructional considerations be applied in the classroom? Imagine presenting a unit on reading informational texts (one supporting the Common Core State Standards) to a typical American public school second-grade reading class: twenty-six students, whose performance levels range from end of kindergarten to end of fourth grade (let's say levels 4 through 40 on the Development Reading Assessment). Planning effective instruction presents a significant challenge. How can we teach students with that range of abilities in a way that is engaging, comprehensible, and appropriately challenging to everyone? I'll be the first to admit it isn't easy, yet I know it can be done.

High Expectations

As Brook explained, high expectations does not mean having the same expectations for all students. But in planning any unit of study, we have to believe in our students' ability to become invested and productive. Either directly or unconsciously, we send messages to children all the time about what we think of them. If we don't believe our students can or will do the work, they won't believe they can do it either. Our job is to check ourselves. What do we believe about our students? We must identify and name students individually, set reasonably high expectations for them, let them know the expectations as plainly and directly as possible, and check in with them frequently.

Here's an example of what I mean. I know there are students who can and must read complex texts about wolves and that they'll be able to have sophisticated discussions. I also know there are students with high oral comprehension skills but much lower reading comprehension. I want to structure some partner reading support so those struggling readers have access to the information necessary to participate in the talk.

I also know there are students who have gaps in their social awareness, which inhibits their ability to explore and debate respectfully. For the first round of discussions, I might give these students a list of talk criteria and ask them to observe what talk moves they see their classmates demonstrating before trying it themselves. The way to set high expectations for all students is to understand their gaps in understanding and competence and then provide the correct support. That way, they all can be achievers.

Opportunities for Active Engagement

I start with giving students some input into the topic we are going to study. Relationships, including student–teacher relationships, are not a do-what-I-say one-way street. I'm very interested in social justice, so I gravitate toward topics that produce discussions about that. For these second graders, I go right to something I know will hook them, animals—even better, endangered ones, in relation to which there is interesting, complicated, and controversial history, both past and present, to discuss. There are also plentiful books (and videos and field trips) at a wide variety of levels to support the study.

We take time to sort through possibilities and agree on a wolf study. The students are invested because they have had a say in what we are doing. Within the topic, I need to create more choice, so we consider areas in which students can decide to become experts:

- wolf packs
- wolf reintroduction in Yellowstone National Park
- wolves as hunters
- red wolves
- gray wolves.

Within each of these subtopics, there are appropriately leveled books for students to read, as well as very kid-friendly videos to watch.

Scaffolded Support

Together, our whole-class lessons are "all about" wolves in the United States, spanning from their near extinction in about 1910 to their reintroduction in 1995. This will allow me to have a justice issue as the thread through our study (extermination and reintroduction) as well as instruction on the features (captions, bold print, subheadings, glossaries, indexes, diagrams) and comprehension of informational texts. Because the topic is new to everyone in the class, the concepts and vocabulary will be challenging for all, but I can provide support with read-alouds and illustrative overheads to show students the text features.

For example, to teach them how to read a diagram, I'll first ask have them participate in an inquiry: *What do they notice? How might they go about making sense of it? What connection do they see between the information in the diagram and the information in the text?* Too often we go right to telling students how to approach the work, and not only are we losing out on an opportunity to assess what scaffolding is necessary, but we are also losing out on an opportunity for engagement—the engagement that comes from teaching students to think. Then, in another lesson, I'll demonstrate how I negotiate and gain information from the diagram. I want to be sure students have this scaffolded support in case they need it. Then they are able to try it on their own, in their own leveled books, and I can both support and push them in conferences.

I'll also work separately with groups of three to six students, teaching strategies they need to negotiate their specific informational texts. At the end of the unit, there will be some things everyone in the class knows about wolves and about informational texts and other things only specific groups know.

Just-Right Challenges

Not too far into the school year, I am expecting the vast majority of second graders to be able to work independently on a task for thirty minutes. Using ideas gleaned from Tony Stead's *Reality Checks*, I teach the students that nonfiction readers often begin reading an informational piece thinking they already know things about a topic. Readers who are really tuned in are able to confirm that information when they come across it or learn that they didn't have it right. Sometimes, however, the thing we think we know isn't mentioned at all.

A couple of weeks into the unit, a number of students absolutely get it. They correct misinformation ("I thought wolves could kill anything they chased, but I learned they only catch prey one out of ten times they try"), learn new information ("No healthy wolf has ever attacked a human"), and raise questions ("Why did humans try to exterminate them and not some other more dangerous animal like a bear?"). They've also devised their own note-taking strategies.

However, students with short attention spans or who struggle with comprehension (especially those with both issues) find this really, really hard. You know those kids—they are the ones who stop working after five minutes and interrupt everyone else, right? We all know those kids. For as bad as they might make us feel because they are interrupting the flow of work, they are probably feeling worse, their behavior the result of feelings of incompetence or boredom at doing the work. A form such as that shown in Figure 5–1 can help students track their thinking. For these students, I divide the thirty-minute work block into two twelve-minute sessions (I have a timer to remind me). I also make sure:

- Students have selected the subtopic—wolf pups.
- The texts are appropriately leveled.
- I've made the table for students so they can't forget the task.
- The task is familiar—they won't get frustrated by it.
- I check in at points to refocus them if necessary.

What we think we know	Yes, we were right	Nope, we were wrong!	Didn't find it!

Figure 5–1. Students Track Their Thinking as They Read an Informational Text

Here's how this support plays out with a group whose subtopic is wolf pups. The first three minutes, I help the students brainstorm what they think they know about pups—we have read about them so they know a lot! When I leave, they write those things down, and then start reading. Twelve minutes later, I check their progress and direct their focus to the remaining aspects of the reality check.

The number of lessons we may need to adjust in a day or the necessity of making adjustments for more than one group can feel overwhelming. But think of it this way: Either we exhaust ourselves planning (at least until it becomes routine), or we exhaust ourselves responding to management issues. In the first instance, the planning becomes easier with practice and we build a positive, caring, supporting relationship with our students. In the second instance, things don't get better, only more frustrating and negative. Whether we are teaching academic or social skills, we need to do so with gradual release in mind.

Opportunities for Social Interaction

The beauty of a study like this is that children get fired up and want to talk. *How could we have tried to exterminate such a magnificent creature? Why is there such bias against the wolf? Why does the wolf represent evil in books? Now that we've brought them back, how will we protect them*? Studies of animals often and easily ignite empathy in children, and I want them to be aware that when they can feel the pain of these animals, they know they are learning something they just have to talk about.

To organize the study, I teach children how to work in groups of four or five and lay out the topic or question they are most heated about. Because an immediate consensus is unlikely, each member of the group writes his or her preference on a sticky note. Then the group members evaluate each suggestion in terms of how much they have to say about it, thereby ending up with the topic that will fuel the meatiest conversations.

Next, I have the group members select two or three texts that will support their discussion. They reread them and highlight parts relevant to their discussion with sticky notes. For example, a group discussing how we should protect wolves in the future would read articles about wolf hunting laws, the Endangered Species Act, and so on.

For the two to three days that follow, students get opportunities to have scheduled discussions. These discussions aren't just about deepening content knowledge or practicing their skills reading informational texts but are opportunities to meet their social needs and teach social skills.

Book talks: The value of structured practice

When we think about social instruction, most of us don't have the time or freedom in schools to think about creating new structures for learning. We need to be able to embed the instruction into structures that already exist. One such structure is read-aloud. We can use that structure to teach children to be better listeners, thinkers, and communicators. We can use read aloud to teach them how to listen, grow ideas, and articulate ideas to a partner and to a large group, as well as to question or embrace what others think and say. We can use read-aloud to give children the communication skills upon which they can have fundamental social needs met.

At the heart of our ability to learn, whether academically, socially, or emotionally, is our ability to communicate. The primary form of human communication is talk. We often think children will learn how to communicate by hearing talk, just as they learned words when they were babies. Not true. They need specific, direct instruction in how to use and interpret language skillfully. Only then can they use it to establish social relationships, make things happen, feel competent, express autonomous thoughts.

Creating safe places for students to talk encourages conversations that are challenging, direct, even emotional. The children aren't afraid to express new thinking or to disagree, just as they aren't afraid to truly listen. We need to give them the tools they need to have meaningful conversations that allow them to know us and one other and share who they are and what they believe. When we teach students how to talk and listen, we are also teaching them self-awareness, self-management, social awareness, and responsible decision making. One of the most natural places to introduce and develop this work is in a read-aloud.

"Turn to a partner and say what you're thinking about the book," I tell my students after I've read aloud a section of Carolyn Coman's *What Jamie Saw* in which Jamie and his mother have a climactic conversation. Kalini and Kayla start right in.

"Ooh! I can't believe Patty just cursed at her son!" gasps Kayla.

"I can't either," Kalani agrees. "See, I told you she was a bad mother. This is just more proof."

"It's true. First she has her kids living with that nasty man, and now she's being so mean to Jamie."

"And he's already flipped out about Van throwing the baby. Now she's just gonna make it worse."

"I think she's really losing control. Thinking she saw Van at the fair flipped her out, and now she thinks Jamie is acting like Van, and she just can't handle that."

"The problem is, it's a mother's job to handle things. She shouldn't be dumping her problems on her children."

This kind of talk should and can be typical in the classroom. Students get to process what they've heard, flesh out ideas, construct new meaning by hearing other ideas, and practice conversation strategies. They get to connect with one another. This is also when I teach students efficacy—using their conversational skills to change others' minds. The social justice issues they read about in books prompt them to imagine a more just world and the stance they might take on behalf of others.

When discussing talk expectations with kids, I used to use the word *accountable*, which is a facet of Lauren Resnick's brilliant work on the principles of learning and leans more toward responsibility. Now I use the word *present*, meaning *I'm right here with you now attending to you and me and this interaction happening between us.* Being present has much more to do with developing the awareness necessary in social and emotional learning.

Some specific tactics we can teach students about talk are listed in Figure 5–2. As you look over these prompts, imagine how they'd be used if children were

What does being fully present look like in a conversation?

» Making natural eye contact: looking at each other, looking away, coming back to look at each other again.

» Waiting for a pause in someone else's speaking before we talk.

» Speaking clearly and at a volume others can hear without straining.

» Leaning in, making facial expressions or gestures to show we are hearing.

When we are fully present in a conversation, our agreements and disagreements are respectful and specific. When we agree:

» I understand what you said about _____ and would like to add _____.

» That makes sense because _____.

» I really connected with that because _____.

» That's true because _____.

» I liked when you said _____ because _____,

When we disagree:

» I don't think that's true because _____.

» I understand what you're saying about _____, but I have a different point of view. I think _____.

» I know that's your opinion, but _____.

» Can you give me evidence to support your opinion?

» I don't agree with your saying _____ because _____.

» I don't think that's true. Can we try to find evidence of that in the text?

When we are fully present we care about what others have to contribute to the conversation. We invite them in and make sure we understand them:

» [Name], it looks like you'd like to say something.

» Can you say more about what you are thinking?

» [Name], if you feel ready to share, I'd love to hear what you think about what I said.

» Can you say that in a different way?

» Let me see if I've got your thinking right. So what you're saying is _____.

» I'm wondering, what makes you think that?

Figure 5-2. Positive Behavior During Conversation

having a disagreement on the playground or if one child felt slighted by another or if one student felt the need to protect another. Imagine conversations you have had with a colleague, a partner, or a friend. Although our focus here is teaching students how to talk during a read-aloud, the skills they are learning are life skills.

Practice makes ~~perfect~~ competent

Student talk during a read-aloud creates a community in which students have a place, show up, are present, and connect with one another. Through careful practice, during which we as teachers notice and name positive behavior, students start to think, "Yes, I can do this." They begin to develop self-confidence about their conversational roles. Following are two snapshots of student talk. One is from early in the school year, one from midyear.

SNAPSHOT 1: OCTOBER

"As you guys are sitting here listening to the Sharon Creech's *The Wanderer*, I can tell you're all hearing and thinking about what I'm reading. You are fully present. Do you know how I can tell? First of all, you're all sitting up with good energy, and you are looking at me, and I'm catching your eyes as I look away from the book during reading. But the way I can really tell you're listening, that you are present, is by looking at your faces while I'm reading. Remember the part of the book when Cody said to the dolphins, 'Hello sweet darlings?'" Heads nod and kids start to smile and giggle. "Well, you did just what you're doing now—you started smiling and giggling. Why did you do that?" Several hands go up.

"Because that was kind of funny, for Cody to do that. He acts all tough and cool all the time, and then he acted all mushy and sweet when he saw the dolphins. It was kind of cute of him, and that's why I laughed."

"And that laugh told me you were really with me, listening to and thinking about what I was reading. It means you're being responsible about learning. You are present. In our classroom, it's really important that we are all learning from each other—I'm not the only person in this room you should be learning from. It is everyone's job in this room to teach each other and learn from each other. One of the easiest ways we can show we're here for each other is through the looks on our faces when we are listening to each other, just like you showed me while I was reading. Anytime anyone in this room is talking, I expect to see you sitting here looking alert, making some eye contact with that person, and showing through the look on your face that you are present and listening."

SNAPSHOT 2: FEBRUARY

At a critical point in *Miracle's Boys*, by Jacqueline Woodson, it is revealed that Milagro (Miracle) was still alive when her youngest son, Lafayette, found her. Until now Lafayette has led everyone to believe that he found her dead, that there was absolutely nothing he could have done to save her. Students are bursting to say something. These are things readers stay with and try to figure out for a long time.

"We've been practicing ways to help those of us who tend to be quiet say more and have deeper involvement in our book talks. Oftentimes people who are quiet are doing some powerhouse thinking, and we want to know it! Today, we are going to make it really smooth for those powerhouse thinkers to share. I've listed some sentence starters [Figure 5–3] that will help bring others into the talk. You'll notice that some of these have blanks in them, and that's where you'd say the person's name. As you're talking in small groups today about why you think Lafayette kept this really shocking piece of information to himself, I'd like those of you who tend to talk a lot in these discussions to try out some of these sentence starters to help get your classmates involved. If you are one of those quiet powerhouse thinkers, you need to push yourselves extra hard to share today. Remember, tone of voice and body language are really important, because the goal is for everyone to feel comfortable about talking. Are there any questions before we get started? Okay, then. I'd like groups of four or five to sit together and talk. Make sure each group includes both girls and boys."

When we are fully present, we care about what others have to contribute to the conversation. We invite them in and make sure we understand them.

» [Name], it looks like you'd like to say something.

» [Name], can you say a little bit more about what you are thinking?

» [Name], let me see if I've got your thinking right. So what you're saying is _____.

» [Name], I'm wondering what makes you think that?

Figure 5–3. Sentence Starters for Helping Others Talk

I spend the first five minutes circulating, noting problems and successes, as well as making recommendations. After another ten minutes, I tell students they have five minutes left in which to finish up their conversation and jot down some thoughts on how things went—problems, successes, what they'd like to try next time. When we reconvene on the carpet, we share what we observed about these group conversations and set new goals. It is also a time for students to openly compliment and critique each other's performance, as well as to publicly set goals.

Inspiring autonomous thought and action

When choosing read-alouds, I try to pick ones on topics or issues students feel strongly about, so they'll want to talk about them. I never pass up an opportunity to expose students to injustice. I want them to notice it at every opportunity and be bothered by it. *How could this be different? Would I participate in this? Stand by and allow this to happen? What will I do some day to make this different?* I'm not just teaching talk for purposes of their relationship with me or with their peers but their relationship with the world.

Here I'll use *Wringer*, Jerry Spinelli at his button-pushing best and an appropriate and engaging read-aloud for fifth grade. The protagonist is a boy named Palmer LaRue. At the annual Family Fest hosted by his town, thousands of pigeons are released and shot. The ten-year-old boys wring the necks of the wounded ones. This year, Palmer's tenth birthday is approaching, and he'll become a "wringer." Things get complicated when shortly before the festival Palmer secretly takes in a pigeon as a pet. The book sparks lots of great conversations for developing activists—about peer pressure, pushing against society's norms, animal rights, and other issues.

While you are teaching students very specific lessons about talk, you are also providing lots of opportunities for self-assessment and peer assessment—that is how you further meet student needs for autonomy while building self-awareness. Examples are provided in Figures 5–4, 5–5, and 5–6.

» What went well in this book talk?

» Was there anything specific that made the conversation get weaker?

» If you could have the conversation again, would you do anything differently?

Figure 5–4. Reflection on Conversation

Who Am I Observing?

Name _____

Conversational Skill	Compliment	Growth Comment
Showed good listening through eye contact and silence		
Showed good listening by restating to make sure he or she heard right		
Showed good listening by adding on		
Showed good listening by asking for clarification		
Showed good listening by circling back to an earlier part of the talk		
Supported talk by referring to specific parts of the text		

Figure 5–5. Peer Assessment

© 2015 by Gianna Cassetta and Brook Sawyer, from *Classroom Management Matters*. Portsmouth, NH: Heinemann.

» How did it feel to observe and give feedback to your peers?

» Was there any feedback you wanted to give but were afraid to?

» What did you see that you would like to try?

» If you participated in the talk, what might you have added?

Figure 5–6. Self-Reflection After Peer Assessment

REFLECTION   What Opportunities Does My Instruction Offer Students?

To see what this might mean for your teaching, take a moment to evaluate one of your lesson plans, ideally one you've taught recently so the details of the interaction are fresh in your mind. (See Figure 5–7.) You've already learned from the research that academic learning and the development of social–emotional skills are linked; focus on what else the students are learning and experiencing besides the day's learning target/standard/objective. Some of these "hidden curricula," the transmission of norms, values, and beliefs in classrooms that reinforce social inequities, occur despite the fact that the teacher believes in education as a vehicle for social justice and equity. Let's see if and where in your lesson plan you are providing students opportunities to practice the behaviors that facilitates their growth.

You probably recognize areas of strength, as well as areas of potential growth. You may also feel some frustration because these ideas are new to you. Remember, this is a different way of evaluating your teaching, and change takes time. Focus on developing one element more deeply in your instruction. For example, in the next week or month, where can you build in meaningful opportunities for social interaction? See which types of social interaction work best, and use them again. Once you feel you have made this adjustment routine, layer on another adjustment next month, and so on.

Students Need the Following Elements of Engaged Instruction	Describe When Students Heard/Experienced This in the Lesson
High expectations	
Just-right challenges	
Scaffolded support	
Opportunities for active participation	
Opportunities for social interaction	

Figure 5–7. Evaluate a Lesson for Elements of Engaged Instruction

© 2015 by Gianna Cassetta and Brook Sawyer, from *Classroom Management Matters*. Portsmouth, NH: Heinemann.

Control What You Can

I've worked with many teachers who feel their hands are tied when it comes to instruction. Sometimes they are partly responsible for the restrictions they feel. After working with a teacher who was conducting a writing workshop, I expressed concern that the students had to do a lot of sitting and listening, and I couldn't tell whether they were understanding the lesson because there was little opportunity to talk. She explained that she was teaching the workshop the way she was told to do it—students only talk during the "active engagement" phase. Although students do talk during that phase of the lesson, she mistook that to mean it was the *only* time.

Many teachers, because they are under pressure, undersupported, and rushed, take at face value what is mandated. It's a fact of life that some of us have more instructional freedom in our classrooms than others. But even in the most highly controlled situations, there's space for us to make adjustments. The decisions we make about academic instruction are directly linked to student behavior, so we need be clear about what is truly off limits. Even if the opportunities are small, let's find ways to use instructional strategies that foster student engagement.

Conclusion

Defining Responsibility

If not us, then who?

If not now, then when?

—JOHN E. LEWIS

A former student, Marco, recently sent me the kind of email we teachers live for. He thanked me for giving him perspective, for helping him see the opportunities in front of him, and for creating a community he still misses. This meant so much to me because my relationship with Marco had not been easy. In the beginning, he questioned everything I did and repeatedly rejected my attempts to connect. And yet, over time I was able to be a steadying presence for Marco. He grew to understand that I knew him well and that I cared about him. I kept showing up, and Marco came to believe that even on days when he wasn't very likeable (or when I wasn't), we'd find our way back to a good relationship.

Why was I able to become such a positive presence for Marco and not one for Frankie (from the Introduction)?

The difference was that I while I continued to engage with Marco, I disengaged from Frankie. I broke the connection, letting Frankie know that I was no longer responsible for him and he was no longer part of the community. I decided his behavior had crossed a line, and by now, you probably know what "the line" means. It reflects the fact that both parties don't have enough tools to connect. The line is not a definition of the limits of our responsibility. The line marks the absence of a sense of capability—"I can't do more; he can't do more." Without that belief in capability, both parties are left disengaged at best, and angry at worst. I am sure you have seen this happen in relationships.

But the cost of disengaging from a child is so great that the balance of obligation lies with us, the adults. When we disengage from a child, we let that child know she or he doesn't belong in our community. What comes of that? Nothing good, whatever the label we choose to rationalize that disengagement. A classroom, a school, a society—these are all communities that become dysfunctional, oppressive in some way, when individuals or groups decide they are no longer responsible for one another.

Every one of us, every day and sometimes multiple times a day, is faced with the choice of whether or not we will be responsible for another. How we respond to that choice is a decision we must each individually own, whether we are subway riders, parents, police officers, and most certainly if we are teachers. When we look at history, it seems as if it is spotted, here and there, with a rare individual who takes responsibility for the good of others—Sojourner Truth, Susan B. Anthony, Gandhi, Martin Luther King Jr.—but I believe that's only the grand part of the picture. Those are the people who were larger than life, who did things so spectacular that we can't help but remember. But that doesn't mean the choices we face are any less important to those whole lives our choices will affect.

Some of us turn our heads, but many of us step up. I know the family who cares for homeless animals until they can be adopted from the local shelter. I know the principal who is a foster parent to the child whose parents have been taken away. I know the students who marched peacefully in unison with the police department to show support for those who lost their lives. I know the teacher who has the "difficult" student stay late as a helper in her classroom each evening until his mom can pick him up from school. Those people will never make it into the history books. But they are out there, right in my neck of the woods, and they have chosen to engage, and be responsible for others. And those whose lives they have touched will never, ever forget them.

My choice with Frankie was to look away, and because of that choice, I know things did not work out well for him. I sometimes look back and wonder, what if I could turn back the clock with Frankie and focus on teaching him what he needed for each day instead of "fixing" him for the long term? What if each day, my work was to give Frankie a small strategy to help him interact more positively and to show him that I noticed his increasing capability? Some might argue that means lowering my expectations, but that's inaccurate. I would have been increasing access through scaffolding toward the same expectation. When we're doing this work, we're helping children realize that they are capable of meeting our expectations with our support. We need to be the bridge to help struggling students find a connection and some success. We can't prevent every student from making bad choices, but we can make sure that they have both a wide array of positive choices they can make and the knowledge that we see the good in them and believe they can do well.

In our relationships with students, our tolerance is continually challenged, and not just by one student, but by many. The difficulty makes the choice to disconnect from them an easy one. In the disconnection, the student feels rejected, incompetent, and incapable. But here's something that's too often overlooked in the dialogue about classroom management: When things go wrong with a student, we feel that way, too. No one wants to be disliked. I have seen many teachers who become someone they never intended because they couldn't move past feeling rejected, incompetent, and incapable. They become calcified in those negative emotions, so that their response to negative experiences is always reactionary and dismissive of criticism. They don't try to connect to every student because it's too risky. They become less than who they could have been in the classroom. And I believe the cost is far greater than that: They become less of who they are in their own lives.

What can happen instead when we expect difficulty and choose to engage anyway? What if we let ourselves acknowledge that some relationships with students won't be easy, but we also promise ourselves that we'll do what's needed to prevent getting stuck in the difficulty? When we don't feel capable, we can reach out to a trusted colleague or a principal or find a helpful book or article. We can engage with the child about what we see and what we expect. We can ask for their input. We can bring ourselves back to research-based practices. But no matter how we handle the situation, we have to uphold our responsibility to our relationship with the child. Disengagement can't continue to be an option. I've shown you many detailed strategies in this book that I hope will prevent and minimize your difficulties with students, but when all else fails, communicating to your student that you believe in your shared capability of something better and pledging to figure out what that better way is . . . well, it can accomplish a lot. Not everything, but a lot.

We don't talk enough about the difficulties of teaching in ways that feel safe. Too often, we worry about appearing weak, vulnerable, incapable. We feel that as teachers, we are supposed to magically have all of the answers. The truth is, even the finest teachers have days or moments when they are bad teachers. When we try to keep our own vulnerability hidden, we're only keeping it hidden from ourselves. I hope that this book is not just a tool for change in individual classrooms but a tool for professional conversation. We need to be able to talk about what makes our job and our students' lives difficult, to cross that difficulty toward greater understanding. We need to be able to talk with others about the difficult and important choices we are faced with in our classrooms about what to emphasize with students and what to teach. And, the better choices we make, the more choices our students have.

At the end of the day, we have to keep making the choice to engage with students no matter what their behavior. Now you have a new set of tools to help you do that. This is your opportunity to be responsible for others—the lasting, positive impact of which you can't even imagine. If you don't do it, who will? If you don't do it now, when will you?

REFERENCES

Ackerman, B. P., E. D. Brown, and C. E. Izard. 2004. "The Relations Between Persistent Poverty and Contextual Risk and Children's Behavior in Elementary School." *Developmental Psychology* 40 (3): 367. doi:10.1037/0012-1649.40.3.367.

Akin-Little, K. A., T. L. Eckert, B. J. Lovett, and S. G. Little. 2004. "Extrinsic Reinforcement in the Classroom: Bribery or Best Practice." *School Psychology Review* 33: 344–62.

Allman, K. L., and J. R. State. 2011. "School Discipline in Public Education: A Brief Review of Current Practices." *International Journal of Educational Leadership Preparation* 6: 1–8.

American Psychological Association. 2008. "Are Zero Tolerance Policies Effective in the Schools? An Evidentiary Review and Recommendations." *American Psychologist* 63: 852–62.

Bambara, L. M., and T. P. Knoster. 2009. *Designing Positive Behavior Support Plans*. 2d ed. Washington, DC: American Association on Intellectual and Developmental Disabilities.

Bandura, A. 1965. "Influence of Models' Reinforcement Contingencies on the Acquisition of Imitative Responses." *Journal of Personality and Social Psychology* 1 (6): 589–95.

Berry-Wilson, M. 2013. *Teasing, Tattling, Defiance and More*. Turners Falls, MA: Center for Responsive Schools.

———. 2014. *The Language of Learning*. Turners Falls, MA: Center for Responsive Schools.

Birch, S. H., and G. W. Ladd. 1997. "The Teacher–Child Relationship and Children's Early School Adjustment." *Journal of School Psychology* 35: 61–79.

Blum, R. W., and H. P. Libbey. 2004. "School Connectedness: Strengthening the Health and Education Outcomes for Teenagers." *Journal of School Health* 74 (4): 229–99.

Bohn, C. M., A. D. Roehrig, and M. Pressley. 2004. "The First Days of School in the Classrooms of Two More Effective and Four Less Effective Primary-Grades Teachers." *The Elementary School Journal* 104: 269–87.

Boxer, P., N. G. Guerra, L. R. Huesmann, and J. Morales. 2005. "Proximal Peer-Level Effects of a Small-Group Selected Prevention on Aggression in Elementary School Children: An Investigation of the Peer Contagion Hypothesis." *Journal of Abnormal Child Psychology* 33 (3): 325–38.

Bullara, D. T. 1993. "Classroom Management Strategies to Reduce Racially-Biased Treatment of Students." *Journal of Educational and Psychological Consultation* 4: 357–68.

CASEL. 2014. "SEL Programs for Elementary School (K–5): Rating Tables." Available at www.casel.org/guide/ratings/elementary.

Cassetta, G., and B. Sawyer. 2013. *No More Taking Away Recess and Other Problematic Discipline Practices*. Portsmouth, NH: Heinemann.

Center, D. B., S. M. Deitz, and M. E. Kaufman. 1982. "Student Ability, Task Difficulty, and Inappropriate Classroom Behavior: A Study of Children with Behavior Disorders." *Behavior Modification* 6 (3): 355–74.

Chin, J. K., E. Dowdy, S. R. Jimerson, and W. J. Rime. 2012. "Alternatives to Suspension: Rationale and Recommendations." *Journal of School Violence* 11: 156–73. doi:10.1080/15388220.2012.652912.

Coman, C. 1997. *What Jamie Saw*. New York: Puffin.

Connell, J. P., and J. G. Wellborn. 1991. "Competence, Autonomy, and Relatedness: A Motivational Analysis of Self-System Processes." *The Minnesota Symposium on Child Development* 43: 43–77.

Conroy, M. A., and W. H. Brown. 2004. "Early Identification, Prevention, and Early Intervention with Young Children at Risk for Emotional and Behavioral Disorders: Issues, Trends, and a Call for Action." *Behavioral Disorders* 29: 224–36.

Coolahan, K., J. Fantuzzo, J. Mendez, and P. McDermott. 2000. "Preschool Peer Interactions and Readiness to Learn: Relationships Between Classroom Peer Play and Learning Behaviors and Conduct." *Journal of Educational Psychology* 92: 458–65.

Creech, S. 2000. *The Wanderer.* New York: HarperTrophy.

Deci, E. L., R. J. Vallerand, L. G. Pelletier, and R. M. Ryan. 1991. "Motivation and Education: The Self-Determination Perspective." *Educational Psychologist* 26: 325–46.

Dishion, T. J., F. Poulin, and B. Burraston. 2001. "Peer Group Dynamics Associated with Iatrogenic Effect in Group Interventions with High-Risk Young Adolescents." *New Directions for Child and Adolescent Development* 2001 (91): 79–92.

Durlak J. A., R. P. Weissberg, A. B. Dymnicki, R. D. Taylor, and K. B. Schellinger. 2011. "The Impact of Enhancing Students' Social and Emotional Learning: A Meta-Analysis of School-Based Universal Interventions." *Child Development* 82 (1): 405–32. doi:10.1111/j.1467-8624.2010.01564.x.

Ebrahim, A. 2012. "The Effect of Cooperative Learning Strategies on Elementary Students' Science Achievement and Social Learning Skills in Kuwait." *International Journal of Science and Mathematics Education* 10 (2): 293–314.

Elias, M. J., and Y. Schwab. 2006. "From Compliance to Responsibility: Social and Emotional Learning and Classroom Management." In *Handbook of Classroom Management: Research, Practice, and Contemporary Issues,* ed. C. M. Evertson and C. S. Weinstein, 309–42. New York: Routledge.

Else-Quest, N., J. Hyde, H. H. Goldsmith, and C. A. Van Hulle. 2006. "Gender Differences in Temperament: A Meta-Analysis." *Psychological Bulletin* 132: 33–72.

Emmer, E. T., C. M. Evertson, and L. M. Anderson. 1980. "Effective Classroom Management at the Beginning of the School Year." *The Elementary School Journal* 80 (5): 219–31.

Epstein, M., M. Atkins, D. Cullinan, K. Kutash, and R. Weaver. 2008. "Reducing Behavior Problems in the Elementary School Classroom: A Practice Guide." NCEE #2008-012. Washington, DC: National Center for Education Evaluation and Regional Assistance, Institute of Education Sciences, U.S. Department of Education. Available at http://ies.ed.gov/ncee/wwc/publications /practiceguides.

Fallon, L. M., B. V. O'Keeffe, and G. Sugai. 2012. "Consideration of Culture and Context in School-wide Positive Behavior Support: A Review of Current Literature." *Journal of Positive Behavior Interventions* 14: 209–20. doi:10.1177/1098300712442242.

Fantuzzo, J., and S. Perlman. 2007. "The Unique Impact of Out-of-Home Placement and the Mediating Effects of Child Maltreatment and Homelessness on Early School Success." *Children and Youth Services Review* 29: 941–60.

Fauth, R. C., J. L. Roth, and J. Brooks-Gunn. 2007. "Does the Neighborhood Context Alter the Link Between Youth's After-School Time Activities and Developmental Outcomes? A Multilevel Analysis." *Developmental Psychology* 43 (3): 760–77. doi:10.1037/0012-1649.43.3.760.

Gay, G. 2006. "Connections Between Classroom Management and Culturally Responsive Reaching." In *Handbook of Classroom Management: Research, Practice, and Contemporary Issues*, ed. C. M. Evertson and C. S. Weinstein, 343–70. New York: Routledge.

Gettinger, M., and K. K. Kohler. 2006. "Process-Outcome Approaches to Classroom Management and Effective Teaching." In *Handbook of Classroom Management: Research, Practice, and Contemporary Issues*, ed. C. M. Evertson and C. S. Weinstein, 73–96. New York: Routledge.

Graziano, P. A., R. D. Reavis, S. P. Keane, and L. D. Calkins. 2007. "The Role of Emotion Regulation in Children's Early Academic Success." *Journal of School Psychology* 45: 3–19. doi:10.1016/j.jsp.2006.09.002.

Greenberg, M. T., R. P. Weissberg, M. U. O'Brien, J. E. Zins, L. Fredericks, H. Resnik, and M. J. Elias. 2003. "Enhancing School-Based Prevention and Youth Development Through Coordinated Social, Emotional, and Academic Learning." *American Psychologist* 58: 466–74.

Hamre, B. K., and R. C. Pianta. 2001. "Early Teacher–Child Relationships and the Trajectory of Children's School Outcomes Through Eighth Grade." *Child Development* 72: 625–38.

Hemphill, S., and J. Hargreaves. 2009. "The Impact of School Suspensions: A Student Wellbeing Issue." *ACHPER Healthy Lifestyles Journal* 56: 5–11.

Hester, P. P., J. M. Hendrickson, and R. A. Gable. 2009. "Forty Years Later: The Value of Praise, Ignoring, and Rules for Preschoolers at Risk for Behavior Disorders." *Education and Treatment of Children* 32: 513–35.

Hinojosa, M. S. 2008. "Black–White Differences in School Suspension: Effect of Student Beliefs About Teachers." *Sociological Spectrum* 28: 175–93.

Hoff, E. 2013. "Interpreting the Early Language Trajectories of Children from Low-SES and Language Minority Homes: Implications for Closing Achievement Gaps." *Developmental Psychology* 49: 4–14. doi:10.1037/a0027238.

Hojnoski, R. L., K. L. Gischlar, and K. N. Missall. 2009. "Improving Child Outcomes with Data-Based Decision Making: Collecting Data." *Young Exceptional Children* 12: 32–44. doi:10.1177/1096250609333025.

Hughes, J. N., W. Lou, O. M. Kwok, and L. K. Loyd. 2008. "Teacher–Student Support, Effortful Engagement, and Achievement: A 3-Year Longitudinal Study." *Journal of Educational Psychology* 100: 1–14. doi:10.1037/0022-0663.100.1.1.

Johnson, D. W., and R. T. Johnson. 2004. "The Three C's of Promoting Social and Emotional Learning." In *Building Academic Success on Social and Emotional Learning*, ed. J. E. Zins, R. P. Weissberg, M. C. Wang, and H. J. Walberg, 40–58. New York: Teachers College Press.

Jones, S. M., and S. M. Bouffard. 2012. "Social and Emotional Learning in Schools from Programs to Strategies." *SRCD Policy Report* 26 (4). Available at http://eric.ed.gov/?id=ED540203.

Justice, L. M., E. A. Cottone, A. Mashburn, and S. E. Rimm-Kaufman. 2008. "Relationships Between Teachers and Preschoolers Who Are at Risk: Contribution of Children's Language Skills, Temperamentally-Based Attributes, and Gender." *Early Education and Development* 19: 600–21. doi:10.1080/104092802231021.

Kamps, D., T. Kravits, J. Stolze, and B. Swaggart. 1999. "Prevention Strategies for at-Risk Students and Students with EBD in Urban Elementary Schools." *Journal of Emotional and Behavioral Disorders* 7: 178–88.

Kern, L., L. Bambara, and J. Fogt. 2002. "Class-Wide Curricular Modification to Improve the Behavior of Students with Emotional or Behavioral Disorders." *Behavioral Disorders* 27: 317–26.

Kern, L., and N. H. Clemens. 2007. "Antecedent Strategies to Promote Appropriate Classroom Behavior." *Psychology in the Schools* 44: 65–75. doi:10.1002/pits.20206.

Klem, A. M., and J. P. Connell. 2004. "Relationships Matter: Linking Teacher Support to Student Engagement and Achievement." *Journal of School Health* 74 (7): 262–73.

Ladd, G. W., S. H. Birch, and E. S. Buhs. 1999. "Children's Social and Scholastic Lives in Kindergarten: Related Spheres of Influence?" *Child Development* 70: 1373–400.

Landrum, T. J., and J. M. Kauffman. 2006. "Behavioral Approaches to Classroom Management." In *Handbook of Classroom Management: Research, Practice, and Contemporary Issues*, ed. C. M. Evertson and C. S. Weinstein, 47–72. New York: Routledge.

Lareau, A. 2011. *Unequal Childhoods: Class, Race, and Family Life.* 2d ed. Berkeley, CA: University of California Press.

Lochman, J. E., R. T. Salekin, and D. A. F. Haaga. 2003. "Prevention and Intervention with Aggressive and Disruptive Children: Next Steps in Behavioral Intervention Research." *Behavior Therapy* 34: 413–19.

Maccoby, E. E. 2004. "Aggression in the Context of Gender Development." In *Aggression, Antisocial Behavior, and Violence Among Girls: A Developmental Perspective*, ed. M. Putallaz and K. L. Bierman, 3–22. New York: Guilford.

Mantzicopoulos, P. 2005. "Conflictual Relationships Between Kindergarten Children and Their Teachers: Associations with Child and Classroom Context Variables." *Journal of School Psychology* 43: 425–42. doi:10.1016/j.jsp.2005.09.004.

Matheson, A. S., and M. D. Shriver. 2005. "Training Teachers to Give Effective Commands: Effects on Student Compliance and Academic Behaviors." *School Psychology Review* 34: 202–19.

Mayer, G. R. 1995. "Preventing Antisocial Behavior in the Schools." *Journal of Applied Behavior Analysis* 28: 467–78.

Montague, M., and C. Renaldi. 2001. "Classroom Dynamics and Children at-Risk: A Follow-Up." *Learning Disability Quarterly* 24: 75–83.

Morine-Dershimer, G. 2006. "Classroom Management and Classroom Discourse." In *Handbook of Classroom Management: Research, Practice, and Contemporary Issues*, ed. C. M. Evertson and C. S. Weinsein, 127–56. New York: Routledge.

Murphy, P. K., I. A. G. Wilkinson, A. O. Soter, M. N. Hennessey, and J. F. Alexander. 2009. "Examining the Effects of Classroom Discussion on Students' Comprehension of Text: A Meta-Analysis." *Journal of Educational Psychology* 101: 740–64. doi:10.1037/a0015576.

National Center for Education Statistics. 2010. "Percentage of Public School Students in Grades 6 Through 12 Who Had Ever Been Suspended or Expelled, by Sex and Race/Ethnicity: 2007." Available at http://nces.ed.gov /pubs2010/2010015/tables/table_17b.asp.

———. 2013. *Condition of Education*. Washington, DC: U. S. Department of Education.

———. 2014. "Back to School Statistics." Available at http://nces.ed.gov/fastfacts /display.asp?id=372.

Normandeau, S., and F. Guay. 1998. "Preschool Behavior and First-Grade School Achievement: The Meditational Role of Cognitive Self-Control." *Journal of Educational Psychology* 90: 111–21.

O'Connor, E., and K. McCartney. 2006. "Testing Associations Between Young Children's Relationships with Mothers and Teachers." *Journal of Educational Psychology* 98: 87–98. doi:10.1037/0022-0663.98.1.87.

Oshima, K., J. Huang, M. Jonson-Reid, and B. Drake, B. 2010. "Children with Disabilities in Poor Households: Association with Juvenile and Adult Offending." *Social Work Research* 34: 102–13.

Patrick, H., J. C. Turner, D. K. Meyer, and C. Midgley. 2003. "How Teachers Establish Psychological Environments During the First Days of School: Associations with Avoidance in Mathematics." *Teachers College Record* 105: 1521–58. doi:10.1111/1467-9620.00299.

Payton, J., R. P. Weissberg, J. A. Durlak, A. B. Dymnicki, R. D. Taylor, K. B. Schellinger, and M. Pachan. 2008. *The Positive Impact of Social and Emotional Learning for Kindergarten to Eighth-Grade Students: Findings from Three Scientific Reviews*. Chicago: Collaborative for Academic, Social, and Emotional Learning.

Pianta, R. C. 1999. *Enhancing Relationships Between Children and Teachers*. Washington, DC: American Psychological Association.

Pressley, M., S. E. Dolezal, L. M. Raphael, L. Mohan, A. D. Roehrig, and K. Bogner. 2003. *Motivating Primary-Grade Students*. New York: Guilford Press.

Qi, C. H., and A. P. Kaiser. 2003. "Behavior Problems of Preschool Children from Low-Income Families: Review of the Literature." *Topics in Early Childhood Special Education* 23: 188–217.

Reeve, J. 2006. "Extrinsic Rewards and Inner Motivation." In *Handbook of Classroom Management: Research, Practice, and Contemporary Issues*, ed. C. M. Evertson and C. S. Weinsein, 645–64. New York: Routledge.

Rhode, G., W. R. Jenson, and D. P. Morgan. 2009. *The Tough Kid New Teacher Book: Practical Classroom Management Survival Strategies*. Eugene, OR: Pacific Northwest Publishing.

Rhode, G., W. R. Jenson, and H. K. Reavis. 1993. *The Tough Kid Book: Practical Classroom Management Strategies*. Longmont, CO: Sopris West.

Richards, L. C., L. T. Heathfield, and W. R. Jenson. 2010. "A Classwide Peer-Modeling Intervention Package to Increase on-Task Behavior." *Psychology in the Schools* 47 (6): 551–66. doi:10.1002/pits.20490.

Roorda, D. L., H. M. Y. Koomen, J. L. Spilt, and F. J. Oort. 2011. "The Influence of Affective Teacher–Student Relationships on Students' School Engagement and Achievement." *Review of Educational Research* 81 (4): 493–529. doi:10.3102/0034654311421793.

Sameroff, A. J., and B. H. Fiese. 2000. "Transactional Regulation: The Developmental Ecology of Early Intervention." *Handbook of Early Childhood Intervention* 2: 135–59.

Shores, R. E., P. L. Gunter, and S. L. Jack. 1993. "Classroom Management Strategies: Are They Setting Events for Coercion?" *Behavioral Disorders* 18 (2): 92–102.

Skiba, R. J., R. H. Homer, C. Chung, M. K. Rausch, S. L. May, and T. Tobin. 2011. "Race Is Not Neutral: A National Investigation of African and Latino Disproportionality in School Discipline." *School Psychology Review* 40: 85–107.

Solomon, D., V. Battistich, M. Watston, E. Schaps, and C. Lewis. 2000. "A Six-District Study of Educational Change: Direct and Mediated Effects of the Child Development Project." *Social Psychology of Education* 4: 3–51.

Spinelli, J. 1997. *Wringer*. New York: HarperTrophy.

Stead, T. 2005. *Reality Checks.* York, ME: Stenhouse.

Stearns, E., K. A. Dodge, and M. Nicholson. 2008. "Peer Contextual Influences on the Growth of Authority-Acceptance Problems in Early Elementary School." *Merrill-Palmer Quarterly* 54 (2): 208–31.

Stormont, M. A., S. C. Smith, and T. J. Lewis. 2007. "Teacher Implementation of Precorrection and Praise Statements in Head Start Classrooms as a Component of a Programwide System of Positive Behavior Support." *Journal of Behavioral Education* 16: 280–90. doi:10.1007/s10864-007-9040-3.

Sullivan, A. L., D. A. Klingbeil, and E. R. Van Nortnan. 2013. "Beyond Behavior: Multilevel Analysis of the Influence of Sociodemographics and School Characteristics on Students' Risk of Suspension." *School Psychology Review* 42: 99–114.

Sutherland, K. S. and J. H. Wehby. 2001. "The Effect of Self-Evaluation on Teaching Behavior in Classrooms for Students with Emotional and Behavioral Disorders." *Journal of Special Education* 35: 161–71. doi:10.1177/002246690103500306.

Thijs, J., and H. M. Koomen. 2009. "Toward a Further Understanding of Teachers' Reports of Early Teacher–Child Relationships: Examining the Roles of Behavior Appraisals and Attributions." *Early Childhood Research Quarterly* 24: 186–97. doi:10.1016/j.ecresq.2009.03.001.

Thompson, G. L. 2007. *Through Ebony Eyes: What Teachers Need to Know but Are Afraid to Ask About African American Students*. San Francisco: Jossey-Bass.

Umbreit, J., J. B. Ferro, C. J. Liaupsin, and K. L. Lane. 2007. *Functional Behavioral Assessment and Function-Based Intervention: An Effective, Practical Approach*. Upper Saddle River, NJ: Prentice-Hall.

Vygotsky, L. S. 1978. *Mind in Society: The Development of Higher Mental Processes*. Cambridge, MA: Harvard University Press.

Waldfogel, J., T. Craigie, and J. Brooks-Gunn. 2010. "Fragile Families and Child Wellbeing." *The Future of Children* 20: 87–112.

Walker, H. M., and R. Sylwester. 1998. "Reducing Students' Refusal and Resistance." *Teaching Exceptional Children* 30: 53–58.

Watson, M., and V. Battistich. 2006. "Building and Sustaining Caring Communities." In *Handbook of Classroom Management: Research, Practice, and Contemporary Issues*, ed. C. M. Evertson and C. S. Weinstein, 253–80. New York: Routledge.

Watson, M., and L. Ecken. 2003. *Learning to Trust: Transforming Difficult Elementary Classrooms Through Developmental Discipline*. Indianapolis, IN: Jossey-Bass.

Wentzel, K. R. 1993. "Does Being Good Make the Grade? Relations Between Academic and Social Competence in Early Adolescence." *Journal of Educational Psychology* 85: 357–64.

Wood, B. K., and J. B. Ferro. 2014. "An Effective Approach to Developing Function-Based Interventions in Early Childhood Classrooms." *Young Exceptional Children* 17: 3–20. doi:10.1177/1096250612451760.

Woodson, J. 2000. *Miracle's Boys.* New York: Speak/Penguin.

Woolfolk Hoy, A., and C. S. Weinstein. 2006. "Student and Teacher Perspectives on Classroom Management." In *Handbook of Classroom Management: Research, Practice, and Contemporary Issues*, ed. C. M. Evertson and C. S. Weinstein, 181–219. New York: Routledge.

Wu, J. Y., J. N. Hughes, and O. M. Kwok. 2010. "Teacher–Student Relationship Quality Type in Elementary Grades: Effects on Trajectories for Achievement and Engagement." *Journal of School Psychology* 48: 357–87. doi:10.1016/j.jsp.2010.06.004.

Zahn-Waxler, C., E. A. Shiftcliff, and K. Marceau. 2008. "Disorders of Childhood and Adolescence: Gender and Psychopathology." *Annual Review of Clinical Psychology* 4: 275–303.